Material History
and Ritual Objects

This edition is dedicated to
Katherine and Arthur, who know
well the dangers of collecting.

Material History and Ritual Objects

George Blake Dexter's
The Lure of Amateur Collecting

Edited and introduced by
Devin Proctor

WESTPHALIA PRESS
An imprint of Policy Studies Organization

Material History and Ritual Objects:
George Blake Dexter's
The Lure of Amateur Collecting

Westphalia Press
An imprint of Policy Studies Organization
dgutierrezs@ipsonet.org

For information:
Westphalia Press
1527 New Hampshire Ave., N.W.
Washington, D.C. 20036

ISBN-13: 978-0944285800
ISBN-10: 0944285805

Updated material and comments on this edition can
be found at the Policy Studies Organization website:
http://www.ipsonet.org/

Original 1923 dust jacket front flap:

THE habit of collecting is one that yields the greatest delight to its possessor, since the collector goes through the world always on the watch for the beautiful and the rare. Because of his taste, he finds his knowledge ever growing, and events and people come to have a deeper significance to him as they are linked up with some exquisite piece of workmanship or something unique in the world of art. But the millionaire collector, who can purchase almost anything he fancies, loses half the zest that comes to the amateur who picks up his treasure here and there as a result of a chance happening or a happy encounter or through some real sacrifice.

Mr. Dexter, through many years of travel through many countries, has obtained a beautiful and unique collection including articles of furniture, porcelains, jewels, plate and souvenirs from celebrities. Each one was acquired as the result of some interesting encounter or experience, and this book tells the stories of these various art objects.

There are stories of chests from Syria and chairs from Italy; tapestries from England; Persian enamels from Thibet; of Colonial Sheffield plate and Chinese porcelains; of Stratford lithographs and Louis XIV's book; of antique Greek gems; of an Irish talisman and an Arabian buckle. From all over the world have come these articles, and the tale of each one strikes either the romantic or dramatic note.

Some of Mr. Dexter's possessions have found their way into the museums, but many others he has retained for his personal enjoyment. The pleasure that went with their attaining, however, can now be shared by all readers of the book.

E

INTRODUCTION
TO THIS EDITION

G EORGE Blake Dexter knew the peril
of indulging in a passion: "One of the
failings of the amateur collector is that
when he possesses one specimen, he
craves more of the same kind; this is
where ... the danger lies, for possession
creates an appetite which is not satisfied
with a duplicate but many more."[i]

In the following book, the reader will
accompany Dexter on escapades of
acquisition, discovering and purchasing
objects of both obsession and whim.
Dexter seems gleefully bent on the
possession of these material objects, and
leaps at any and every opportunity to
attain them. To possess an object,

according to Jean Baudrillard, one must divest it of its intended purpose. "An object no longer specified by its function is defined by the subject, but in the passionate abstract-ness of possession all objects are equivalent. And just one object no longer suffices." [ii] Collection begets possession begets collection ad infinitum. This is precisely *The Lure of Amateur Collecting* that George Blake Dexter speaks to in this book.

Dexter, a 'Boston Brahmin,' born into an advantaged and patrician lineage, relates his adventures, from those in his childhood, travelling with his family in Europe, to those of an adult with full access to worldwide markets. His passion for collection and possession is evident throughout the book, with anecdotes spanning from the 1870s into the early 1920s full of humor, surprise, and more than a few celebrity cameos. Dexter does more in the book than showcase his extensive material collection, however; this memoir itself serves as a ritual object for the possession of the circumstances of his findings. It allows for the collection of memories. As Walter Benjamin has said, "every passion borders on the chaotic, but the collector's passion borders on the chaos of memories."[iii] In writing down his stories of adventurous procurement, Dexter has also collected his own past, and given order to the chaos of memories.

Readers will react to Dexter and this work in different ways, to be sure. He was not at all reluctant to regale anyone who would listen regarding his achievements. As Professor Beverly Gordon has pointed out, "Dexter's self-aggrandizing exploits did not end with procuring these exotic items; he seems to have made a career of speaking about these adventures at places like the National Arts Club and war charity efforts."[iv] It would be easy to brush off the stories contained in this book as an ego trip of the privileged class, but there is more to be learned herein than that.

Our current popular culture has a conflicted obsession with the possession and collection of material objects. One only needs to look at television programming: on one hand, collection is demonized in some shows and referred to as hoarding, revealed as a mental illness; on the other hand, some shows valorize the practice of 'antiquing' or 'picking' and portray practitioners as expert historians of material antiquity who should be rewarded handsomely.

Similarly, we may view Dexter himself with such conflict. We may cringe when he speaks of business relations with a "wily old Chinaman," and of "this 'white' Jew." We may be appalled when he greets a devastating cholera epidemic in Syria with satisfaction, as it will lower his importing fees. We may read the entire

I

manuscript as an exercise in Orientalist commodity fetishism. We may also be swept away by old-world adventure, and contextualize the more problematic aspects of the language as a quaint indication of the era. Or we may, like Professor Gordon, simply be annoyed at his grating self-indulgence.

However we react, it must be argued that the book is an entertaining window into a world few of us will ever hope to know. How many of us truly have the ability or access to fully immerse ourselves in our passions, as George Blake Dexter could? All told, even after his countless bequeathals to museums, this collection of memories may be his greatest gift to posterity.

Devin Proctor

J

[i] Pg. 68

[ii] Jean Baudrillard, *The System of Objects*, Verso, London, 2005.

[iii] Walter Benjamin, *Illuminations: Essays and Reflections*, Harcourt Brace Jovanovich, 1968.

[iv] Beverly Gordon, *The Saturated World,* University of Tennessee Press, 2006.

K

THE LURE OF AMATEUR
COLLECTING

SHEFFIELD PLATE

THE LURE OF
AMATEUR COLLECTING

BY
GEORGE BLAKE DEXTER

WITH ILLUSTRATIONS

To
MY WIFE

PREFACE

AT the University Club in New York
in 1915 four gentlemen who were all
interested in the same hobby sat at luncheon.

They were all amateur collectors of beautiful objects. It was their purpose to tell of
the experiences in foreign travel during many
years and how each had become possessed
of rare gems and furniture. The hours quickly
passed and at five o'clock in the afternoon
they went downstairs and separated.

"Will you come to the National Arts Club
next Monday evening, to the men's open
table, and bring some of the small objects
you have told about to-day, and talk about
the different gems and books?" inquired one
of these gentlemen of his companion, as they
sauntered down Fifth Avenue.

"Gladly, if you think the men would be
interested. Of course, it would simply be a
conversational talk; and the only dread I

should have would be the fear of being thought egotistical. One cannot relate such experiences without bringing the personal pronoun into them rather often, where the stories cover fifty years or more of travel and collecting," answered the other man, — myself.

Being assured that the experiences would be well received, I consented to be there on the following Monday evening.

At that dinner at the National Arts Club and to the eighty-two men who sat at the tables and listened so kindly to my stories I shall always feel deeply grateful, for it was the kind reception I had that evening that tempted me later to accept the many invitations from clubs and societies to repeat my talk for the benefit of the War Charities during the following five years. Now I have been persuaded to relate them with illustrations in book form, hoping some other person may embrace the habit of collecting as a great source of pleasure to himself and others.

One does not travel for pleasure into many countries without making friends and acquaintances and having surprising things happen, unless one keeps to one's self and makes it impossible for others to approach one. I must confess to possessing a happy disposition and in all the years of travel to meeting only kindness and regard from fellow travelers.

In relating these tales I refrain from the mention of the names of any persons who are living, although I know it would give more quality to the stories, but at the same time it might cause embarrassment to some person who had been kindness itself to me.

Undoubtedly the man who collects for the millionaire collector has the fun of it, with all its thrills, while the rich man, who because of his pile of gold is able to own objects of art, has only the gratification of ownership and the final satisfaction of giving his treasures to a museum to perpetuate his name; — but the first man, who may never be heard of in connection with these same treasures, is able to recount to his intimates with great satisfaction the story of how he was able to secure some of the choice specimens of the millionaire's wonderful collection.

In choosing the pieces of my small col-

lection which seem to me to have the most
interesting anecdotes connected with them,
I realize how much the illustrations add, and
I therefore acknowledge my indebtedness to
the Museum of Fine Arts in Boston and Mr.
E. J. Moore, the Museum photographer,
for the rendering of the illustrations.

BOSTON, May, 1923   G. B. D.

CONTENTS

ILLUSTRATIONS

THE LURE OF
AMATEUR COLLECTING

THE LURE OF AMATEUR COLLECTING

CHAPTER 1

HOW THE COLLECTION STARTED

THE FRANCO–PRUSSIAN War was just closing when my uncle and I, a boy fifteen years of age, arrived in London. Everything was fairyland to my youthful mind.

After a few days in London my uncle left me alone in the Golden Cross Hotel, Charing Cross, and went north to complete some business arrangements. As I look back now over fifty years I cannot understand his leaving me at that age in a city where I knew no one. He intended to be away two weeks and stipulated that I should not go out of the hotel alone after six o'clock in the evening.

It was the month of June and rained almost every day. Therefore I was obliged to amuse myself indoors. Having a sketch-book with me, I used to sit at my bedroom door and sketch the hallway with the staircase at the farther end and try to get the perspective correct in my drawing-book. One morning a Frenchman came down the hall and looking over my shoulder said, "Ah, you sketch. My master is an artist. Let me show him your book." So off he went to a room at the end of the hall.

Presently he returned and said, "My master says if you want to come into his room, you may try to copy some of his black-and-white sketches he has made of London."

In entering the room I met another Frenchman who spoke very little English. He gave me some drawing paper and charcoal, also some of his sketches, and told me to lie on the floor and copy them.

This went on for several days. One afternoon "the master" (that was the only name I knew for him) said through Jacques, the valet, that he was going to sketch Old Billingsgate Market the next morning at daybreak, and if I would like to go, I could accompany him in the four wheeler and Jacques would go in a

hansom cab with the easel and other para-
phernalia.

The next morning when we reached the
market, we found the fish were in pens separated by fences but there were no aisles, so
that to reach the stools that had been placed
for "the master" to sketch from we had to be
carried on the backs of men who waded through
the fish. The women who were selling the fish
had their skirts fastened very high on their
hips and made their way through the market
with bare legs and feet.

The lights or lanterns which hung by iron
chains made great spots of light in the otherwise gloom which particularly appealed to
the artistic sense of an artist in black-and-
white. The sketches were mere marks without
shading and written suggestions, all worked
up afterward in the studio into the wonderful
black-and-white pictures.

There were many excursions of this kind
on which I was permitted to go.

One day "the master" said he was going
to sketch Temple Bar. He loved riding on
the top of a London bus, so this morning,
instead of getting off at Fleet Street, we went

on to the end of the route and got off on the
return trip. He made me sit beside the driver
while he sat just behind us and listened to
our conversation. Although he could not
speak English, he could understand it.

One driver in particular was a character.
Seated on his seat with his high, broad, bell-
shaped gray hat pulled down to the top
of his ears, and his heavy overcoat collar
turned up to meet the hat, he remarked,
"Lord Roseberry rides twice a week with
me and, knowin' I talks with everybody,
gets my views on politics, and in that way
gets the views of the people. Then he takes
them over to Parliament."

Another day "the master" took me to the
Imperial Hotel and into a huge room furnished
like a studio, containing many large pictures. I wandered around the room while
"the master" talked with two gentlemen, one
a large man, and the other small and thin.
On the way home he said the gentlemen were
Mr. Gladstone and Dean Stanley. At that
time I supposed he went as others did to
view the pictures.

At the end of the two weeks' absence, I

received a telegram from my uncle, telling me to have my trunk packed and my bill paid and meet him that afternoon at four o'clock in the Charing Cross station, as we were leaving immediately for the Continent.

Of course, to a boy of fifteen it was a great moment, and I rushed to "the master's" room to impart the news and say good-by.

"The master" asked if we were going to Paris. I told him I did not think so, but we would go to Brussels and later to Bordeaux, avoiding Paris on account of the "Commune", which made Paris unsafe at that time. He then told me if we did go to Paris, to be sure to go to see the Arc de Triomphe and the bas-relief of the woman with the flag leading the soldiers.

He said, "That bas-relief is the best piece of French sculpture of the century, done by François Rode in 1835." Promising to go to see it, I was leaving the room when he called me back, and out of his trunk he took a small leather case containing a gilt copper medal. As he passed it to me he told me it was one of the medals which Louis Philippe gave his twenty ministers at the unveiling of the Arc de Triomphe in 1836. On one side is the head of the Emperor and the reverse side bears a bas-relief of the Arc de Triomphe.

The medal was beautifully modeled by Montagny, the foremost medal sculptor of the time.

I thanked him, boy fashion, and as I took it from him he placed a small photograph of himself and his visiting card with the case and tied a ribbon around them.

I met my uncle and we journeyed to Brussels. The next evening he asked me what I had been doing during the two weeks in London and I told him about the artist. When he asked me who the man was, I said I only knew him by the name of "master." He sent me to my room for the medal. When he untied the ribbon, the visiting card fell to the floor and on reading it he exclaimed, "Gustav Doré!"

Months after, on returning to London, I found that the great studio in the Imperial Hotel was M. Doré's, and the pictures on the walls were his. Then I learned that he would often absent himself for two weeks at a time and go back to his old room in the Golden

LOUIS PHILIPPE MEDAL

Cross Hotel, which he formerly occupied in 1869 when he first came to London and was in moderate circumstances.

The Doré Gallery on Bond Street had been opened in 1869 and was one of those most frequented by Londoners and travelers; but in 1922 I traversed the length of Bond Street in search of it. Alas, it was no more!

Southerby has the building and upon inquiry for the Doré pictures, all the young woman in charge could tell me was that the pictures had vanished and no one in any of the galleries in Bond Street could say what had become of them. The guidebooks make no reference to the Doré Gallery.

Such is fame!

CHAPTER II

A SOUVENIR FROM ROYALTY

AT the time I was left alone in London in June, 1871, in the Golden Cross Hotel, Charing Cross, I looked out of the window facing Charing Cross Station one day and saw a crowd of people all trying to enter the station. Wondering what was the cause of the excitement I went to the street and inquired of a policeman. He told me that Frederick, the Crown Prince of Prussia, was arriving with his wife, Queen Victoria's eldest daughter, the first visit since the Franco-Prussian War, and that the Royal Family, with the exception of the Queen, were in the station awaiting the arrival.

Naturally an American boy of fifteen who had never seen royalty was much interested, and I confided in the "bobby" and asked how I could get into the station. He suggested that I try the hotel above the station.

I suppose a boy of fifteen can worm his way through a densely thick crowd easier than any other creature. Soon I found myself inside the hotel, ascending the stairs, which were also crowded.

In the corridor above I interviewed the hotel porter and told him I was an American boy and had never seen royalty and implored him to assist me. He pointed down the corridor and said, "if you can get through that small door at the end without my seeing you, you will find a circular iron staircase which leads down into a passageway from the front to the interior of the station."

I backed toward the door, keeping my eyes on the porter, and then suddenly, when he was not looking, I popped inside the door and closed it after me. A single gas jet was burning and disclosed the iron circular staircase. I went down the stairs and found the passageway carpeted with red baize carpeting.

Two ladies from outside passed me as I reached the floor and then a gentleman in a tall silk hat and a Prince Albert coat put his hand on my shoulder and said, "Who are you? Where did you come from?"

I said, "I am an American boy and never have seen royalty, so I came down this way from the hotel."

He laughed and pushed me ahead of him, and presently we were in the station where thousands of people were behind red ropes on either side. Just inside the doorway we had entered stood a gentleman in waiting and a boy about my own age. The gentleman who had pushed me ahead of him said to the gentleman in waiting, "Here's an American boy who has never seen royalty," and went on his way, laughing.

The boy standing there looked at me and exclaimed, "Don't put him into the crowd. He will not see a thing. Let him stand here beside you."

"Very well," replied the gentleman, and as the boy left us I was conscious of occupying a superior position.

Presently the train arrived and amid the cheers of the great crowd the ladies and gentlemen of royalty came toward the door where I was allowed to stand. I remember as a boy how surprised I was to see the same affection displayed among these people as we ordinary mortals show in welcoming our relations.

The last to pass me was the boy. He asked if I had seen everything and after I had thanked him, he said, "Have you been out to Windsor Castle yet?" — and when I told him I had not, he replied, "You ask this gentleman for his card and when you come he will send for me and I'll show you through the Castle."

When he had gone the gentleman turned and gave me his card and asked me if I knew who the boy was; I replied in the negative, but he offered no information.

Two days after that being a pleasant day, I went to Windsor. Inside the Castle gate I presented the gentleman's card and was directed to the offices of the household. From one room to another I was passed, until I came to the room in which the man I was in search of sat at a desk. He looked up and remarked, "You did not lose any time in getting out here."

I suppose now he meant this as a pleasantry, but I did not appreciate it at the time.

" You sit down and I will send for the boy."

It was some time before the boy arrived.

"I'm glad to see you," he greeted me. "We'll not go and join the people who are going through the Castle with guides. Come through here," — and we were immediately in the great staircase hall.

I do not suppose two boys ever went through Windsor Castle as we did. We rushed from one part to the other, and I did not really see a thing.

At last he said, "You ever seen Eton where the boys all go to school?" And upon my saying that I had never been out there before, he opened a door which was under the great stone staircase, — a carriage entrance.

There stood a pair of ponies in a phaeton and a man sitting in the rumble behind.

"I'm going to drive you down to Eton. It's only a few miles."

He took the reins and told me to "pile in."

All the way to Eton the boy talked about America and the Indians. He said he had been reading Fenimore Cooper's books and asked me if we saw many Indians in Boston.

When we reached the Castle again, after driving through the Park as far as Virginia Waters, I said I must be getting back to London to lunch, and he said he must go to lunch too.

"You give me your father's name and address in Boston, and when I come over I'll hunt you up and we will go out West and see the Indians."

I asked him his name.

He said, "They call me Leopold."

Telling me to wait, he left me, and, after fifteen minutes had passed, he came back and gave me a miniature Dresden cup and saucer, saying, "I tried to find something to give you to remember me with, but I could only find this girl thing — "

I took it, and have it still unbroken after fifty years. On the underside of the cup and saucer are the initials A. R. Sixty years ago Augustus, King of Saxony, had his initials of "Augustus Rex" put on all Dresden china he gave to other royalty.

In 1914 my wife and daughters and I visited again Windsor Castle; going through St. George's Chapel, we came into Prince

Albert Chapel, and there on a catafalque of stone is a recumbent figure of a man in Highland costume who died thirty years before at thirty years of age, and on the stone is carved

LEOPOLD

DUKE OF ALBANY

YOUNGEST SON OF QUEEN VICTORIA

Two boys, — one who wanted to see Indians and one who wanted to see royalty!

This year (1922), being in London again, I asked at the Charing Cross Hotel to see the door on the second floor through which, fifty-one years ago, I passed to find the iron circular stairs which led to the passage below. The manager said that he knew of no such stairs, but added that he had only been there twenty-five years. He called an old porter who listened to my story and then turning to the manager said, "Yes, the gentleman is quite right. About thirty years ago the passageway was widened and made into a carriage entrance and the stairs are still there, making the lower part of the fire escape from

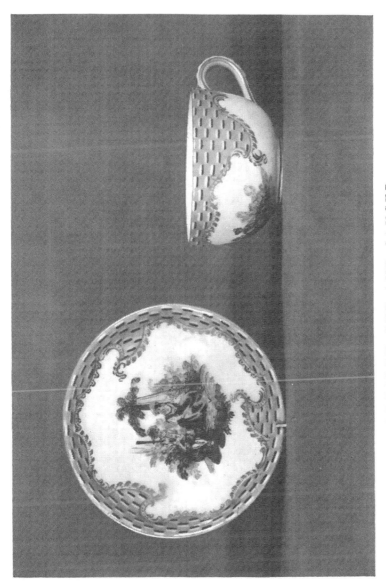

DRESDEN CUP AND SAUCER

above." So my youthful adventure was confirmed.

The door at Windsor Castle under the Grand Staircase is still there, opening under a *porte-cochère* upon the quadrangle where the ponies attached to the phaeton stood.

CHAPTER III

BONAPARTE'S LETTER

IN Oxford, in 1913, a friend told me of an old man who had a wonderful collection of prints, books and autographs stored in the attic rooms of his house and suggested that I make his acquaintance and gain access to the attic, a privilege which he granted collectors (if he took a fancy to them). I thought it all over and finally decided to go directly to the old gentleman and ask if I could inspect his collection.

When I called on him, he was puzzling over a faded letter he held in his hand. There was no need of an introduction, as he simply passed me the old letter and asked, "What do you make out of this?"

It was without date, but written in French and signed Bonaparte. When folded, as in the days before envelopes came into use, it was addressed in another handwriting to

Major Heyles,
        3 Rue de Pyramide,
                Paris,

and bore the postmark Paris, August, 1830, the date on which it was mailed to Major Heyles, nine years after Napoleon's death.

I knew the handwriting of Napoleon Bonaparte and was convinced that he had not written the letter.

Translated it read as follows:

I have read your letter and thank you for having written me.

You should not desire your return to France.

You would have to march over one hundred thousand dead bodies. Sacrifice your interests to the peace and happiness of France.

History will hold you responsible.

I am not insensible to the misfortunes of your family;

I will contribute with pleasure to the peace and tranquillity of your retreat.

(Signed) Bonaparte.

Mr. R—— (the old gentleman) said if I would go to a certain number on Iffly Road and interview a young student who lived there, he would tell me about finding the letter and perhaps would sell it to me, as he, Mr. R——, did not care for it.

At the house in Iffly Road I found the young student, who said that Major Heyles was connected with the British Embassy in Paris in 1830 and was a collector of autographs. At seventy years of age he came back to England and married a young woman not thirty years of age. This young woman was afterward the godmother of the young man. A few months before, in 1913, she had passed away, leaving the military chest of her late husband with its contents to this young man. In a secret drawer he had found a number of valuable autograph letters which he had sold. This one signed "Bonaparte" no one would buy.

Seeing he was anxious to turn the letter into money, and feeling that there was just enough mystery in the letter to make the possession of it interesting, I decided to buy it. We came to terms, and I left him, after receiving a written account of how he came by the chest and letter.

Several months after that, while in Paris, I showed the letter to a friend of mine connected with the Bibliothèque Nationale and asked his opinion of it.

After much deliberation he exclaimed, "When Napoleon Bonaparte was away from Paris, the eldest Bonaparte remaining in Paris always signed himself Bonaparte. Now Louis Bonaparte had abdicated the throne of Holland in favor of his son and was in Paris at the time Napoleon was at Elba. Napoleon Bonaparte wrote to his brother Louis Bonaparte asking his opinion about his (Napoleon) returning to Paris (which letter is now in the archives in Paris), and this was the answer from Louis Bonaparte."

I was later offered such a large sum for the letter that I was convinced it was an original. Some one, knowing Major Heyles collected interesting letters, mailed this to him in 1830, nine years after Napoleon's death, and then almost a hundred years after, the chest gave forth its treasure and I took it back to Paris. I was taken to the room of facsimiles of letters and documents and shown the signatures of Louis Bonaparte, which were the same as the one on the letter I possessed.

CHAPTER IV

THE STRATFORD LITHOGRAPHS

NOW to go back to the old gentleman in Oxford who first showed me the Bonaparte letter.

On a subsequent visit to him he accompanied me to the attic of his house which was stored with prints, books and china. He left me alone, saying that anything I found interesting he would price later.

Among other things was a long tin tube with a cover over the unsealed end. It contained lithographic illustrations of paintings discovered on the walls of the Holy Trinity Chapel at Stratford-on-Avon in 1804. The first part was published in 1807 by one Thomas Fisher of Hoxton, England, one of the best engravers of his time. In 1807, upon the completion of his first lithographic plates, of which there were to be but one hundred and twenty copies, the new Copy-

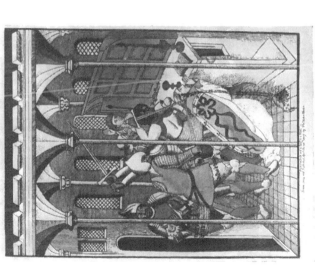

FRESCOES OF THE MURDER OF THOMAS A BECKET ALSO ST. GEORGE
AND THE DRAGON
Chapel of the Trinity, Stratford-on-Avon

right Act became law; this required eleven books of the publication, almost a tithe of the whole, to be given to State libraries. Mr. Fisher became discouraged and suspended his labors, only a few copies of his drawings having been published before the engraved stones were destroyed. Fisher died in 1836, and one Nichols, from a set of the original publication, reproduced a volume which may be found on sale or in libraries in England to-day, but of the original publication of 1807, as far as I can discover, only a few copies are in existence. The Librarian of the Bodleian Library at Oxford writes me that they have not the original edition, and I find them only in the British Museum and the London Institution (Finsbury Circus) and in the libraries of Mr. Huntington and Mr. Folger in New York, and this one which was in the tin box in the Oxford house attic. Mr. R—— did not know where he procured it, and not until after I had made the purchase and taken the set to London did I realize what a treasure I had.

The description of some of the paintings I take from the edition published in 1836.

PLATE XIV:

"This picture, the situation of which at the West end of the nave of the Chapel is denoted in the plan, represents the murder of St. Thomas à Becket. The Archbishop had taken refuge in his Cathedral Church at the altar of St. Benedict, which is here represented as furnished with two lighted tapers in cuplike candlesticks, a missal, and a chalice. The manner in which the assassins approach corresponds exactly with the accounts given by the chronicles, though their military costume is more of the time of the painting than that of the event.

"As the black-letter inscription denotes, William de Tracy and Reginald Fitzurse were the knights who struck the first blows; almost at the same time; then followed Hugh Morville; and lastly Richard Brito. Behind is the faithful clerk, Edmund Grim, whose arm was nearly cut off in endeavouring to ward off the blow of the first assassin, William de Tracy."

Beneath the martyrdom of Becket were painted these verses·

Who so him bethought
Inwardly and oft
How hard it is to fit
From bed to pit,
From pit to pain
That never shall cease certain,
He would do no sin
All the world to win.

PLATE XVII:

"This subject, like that of the Murder of
Becket, was one which was a great favorite
in England, the Combat of her tutelar patron,
Saint George, with the fierce and relentless
dragon; a design at first allegorical of the
Christian's warfare with his spiritual enemy,
but afterwards amplified in the legends into
a long and romantic story (adapted it may be
thought from that of Perseus in Ovid), all
the accessories of which were inserted into
the paintings of a later period as in the in-
stance before us.

"The victory is here represented more than
half accomplished; for the monster is pierced
through the neck by the spear, though it
has subsequently seized the shaft, and broken
it with its claws.

"The Saint is now returning to the charge, sword in hand, and the horse has just struck the dragon's mouth with the point of its frontal or champfrein, which gives the noble steed the appearance of an unicorn. In the background is the devoted Princess with her virgin hair dishevelled, and a lamb her companion, the emblem of her purity and innocence. Her royal parents are anxiously watching her fate, from the gates of the City of Silence, which is here represented as a seaport."

Plate XIX:

"The large painting, which was in full view of the nave, above the chancel arch, represents the Last Judgment or Day of Doom.

"In the center is the Almighty seated on a bow, between Saint Mary and Saint John, who are kneeling in adoration. In the front are persons of both sexes, and of various ranks, rising from their graves; and among them are a Pope distinguished by his tiara, a King by his crown, a Bishop by his mitre, and Monks by their tonsure. On the right hand

FRESCOES OF THE JUDGMENT DAY AND
SEARCH FOR THE HOLY CROSS
Chapel of the Trinity, Stratford-on-Avon

of the Almighty are the Mansions of Heaven, represented as a city, with a giant figure of St. Peter receiving the righteous at the gate. On the opposite side are the wicked being turned into hell, its entrance represented, as was usual, by the mouth of a devouring monster: and within its fiery gulph they are suffering various torments from the busy demons. Some of the figures are marked with labels denoting Pride, Avarice, Wrath, Envy, Gluttony; two more, Sloth and Lechery (the names of which have perhaps been defaced) would complete the number of the Seven Deadly Sins reckoned by the Church of Rome. On the battlements of Hell are some demoniac trumpeters, reminding the spectator of the old line, 'Beware of the devil, when he blows his horn,' but on the opposite turrets it will be perceived there is more varied and more delightful melody."

On these frescoes William Shakespeare must have gazed whenever he attended services at Trinity Church. It is supposed that during Cromwell's time the frescoes were covered with whitewash and forgotten until they were discovered in 1807. After these lithographic copies were made, the walls were all repainted in plain oil colors.

It seems incredible that only about one hundred and twenty years ago when the frescoes were discovered that any Church vestrymen could have had them destroyed. Ten years ago I wrote to the clerk of Trinity Church at Stratford-on-Avon and inquired if they possessed even the reproductions of the lithographs of these frescoes and he replied that they did not or the library of Stratford did not have a copy even of those published in 1836.

CHAPTER V

LOUIS XIV'S CRYPTOGRAM

IN Brussels, November, 1913, a Belgian friend of mine told me of an old French library which was going to be sold at auction, but as the date of the sale was two weeks later than we were planning our stay in Brussels, my friend procured a card which permitted me to look over the books.

The old man who had charge of the library gave me prices at private sale, so I was able to procure ten interesting volumes. Among them was a small book bound in the original vellum. It was printed in Amsterdam, 1648, and written by Thomas Farnabi, an Italian who lived in London in the middle of the seventeenth century, and wrote satires in English on Virgil, Homer, Perseus and others. These satires were translated into different languages and were some of the silly books which were read in the Courts of Europe.

This particular book was translated into Latin. The copper-plate frontispiece attracted my attention at first. It was of tragedy and comedy and beautifully etched, so I bought it.

That evening, as we were examining the books, my wife remarked that the fly leaves of the Farnabi book were pasted together around the edges. Some one said that this was frequently done at the time of the French Revolution. A man about to be executed and having no opportunity to talk to his family, remembering that he had books with valuable autographs in them, would seal the edges with a little flour paste, hoping that later his relatives would discover the autograph.

My wife took a dinner knife and opened the sealed pages, and there, in faded ink, was the name

Louis Soleil

1684

with a cryptogram in old Latin underneath, in another handwriting. I could not believe that I had an autograph of Louis XIV, but the date 1684 was the height of his reign. As we were going to Paris in a few days, I decided to wait and see what they said about it there.

After reaching Paris I took the little book to the Bibliothèque Nationale. One of the curators who had given me some advice before was much interested and took me to the facsimile room where the reproductions of all the documents signed by Louis XIV were kept. All the signatures on public documents were much larger than in my little book, and the "Louis" was an inch or inch and a half in length: but when reduced by a minimizing glass it was exactly like mine in formation.

The curator seemed much interested and left the room for a while, returning with a book, "The history of Madame de Maintenon." In this was the account of Madame de Maintenon when governess to the children in Louis XIV's family. She became enamored of Louis and in 1678 used to call him Louis of the Sun. After that, all his portraits at Fontainebleu had the golden sun painted behind him, and all the pictures

of him on the wall of Versailles have the sun
in gold.

In 1683 the Empress became ill and died,
and at Christmas time the same year Madame
de Maintenon was married privately to Louis
and went to the palace to live. The little
book is dated 1684 under the autograph.

The curator could not read the old Latin
cryptogram. I brought it to Boston and Mr.
Swift at the Public Library, also unable to
read the cryptogram, sent me to a certain
professor at Harvard. He deciphered it at
once:

"If you know who was called Soleil
you know who signed the book."

A well-known firm in London have sent
their representative in New York to see the
little book. He said, "It is the only signature
we know of where Louis XIV signed himself
'Louis Soleil.'" He named so large a sum
which the firm would offer for it that I was
staggered.

In this same library in Brussels was a
curious old parchment with a black wax seal
hanging to it by a ribbon of parchment.

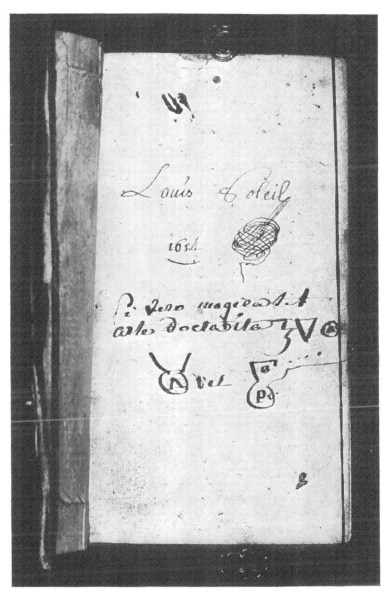

LOUIS XIV AUTOGRAPH
Seventeenth Century Book

It was written in old Flemish, when writing
was an art and was beautifully rendered. The
document bore the date of 1580. The collector said he could not read old Flemish and
named a low price if I cared to purchase it.
I passed it by, and yet it made an impression
on my mind; after several weeks I arrived
at Antwerp and visited that wonderful museum known as the Musée Plantin-Moretus
where everything that was best in the printers'
and engravers' art during the seventeenth
and eighteenth centuries is exhibited. I
found in a glass case on the lower floor three
parchments with seals attached like the one I
had seen in Brussels. I inquired about them
and was told that the curator was the only
one who knew their history. He was most
courteous and explained that the three parchments in the glass case in the museum were
the oldest deeds extant of any buildings in
Antwerp, and the seal was the aldermanic
seal of the city in the sixteenth century.

When I said, "I know where there is one
for sale," he looked incredulous and answered,
"I should like to see it." I promised to show
it to him within a few days.

That afternoon I wrote a friend in Brussels, who was with me when the parchment was shown, and asked him to purchase and mail it to me. The third day after, the document was in my hands in Antwerp.

When the curator saw it, he exclaimed, "Yes, it is an original. I should like to have it for a few days and translate it. I want to call your attention to one thing. The aldermanic seal on your document is perfect, while those on ours are all more or less broken."

Later he restored the deed to me, saying that it was a deed of one of the houses in the square in front of the great Cathedral. He said, "The date of the deed, 1580, was a perilous time in the history of Antwerp. The Cathedral had been completed only about forty years. Four years previous to the writing of the deed the Spanish soldiers had plundered Antwerp and killed six thousand people and burned eight hundred houses. Possibly this deed was for one of the newly constructed houses. Five years later, 1585, the Duke of Parma captured the city and drove every Protestant into exile."

When one realizes this document was written and signed forty years before the Pilgrims landed at Plymouth, over three hundred and forty years ago, we can see how wise the people were to use parchment instead of paper for documents they wished to preserve.

This deed, with its aldermanic seal, is now to be sent to the Musée Plantin-Moretus, as it belongs there.

CHAPTER VI

THE CROSS OF ST. ANNE

IN 1871 I left Glasgow to go through the Trossachs. Being a small boy, I was given a seat in a covered carriage instead of a seat in the great coach drawn by four horses. This was a great disappointment to me.

The carriage was occupied by Lord A—— and his three homely old-maid daughters, who looked me over scornfully, and I was conscious from the first that they did not approve of anything American and least of all an American boy traveling alone. My uncle had planned to meet me on the following Sunday at the Great Western Hotel in Oban, Scotland.

As our horses pulled us up one hill after another, my eye caught sight of beautiful ferns and since I was provided with a tin fern box and a trowel I jumped out of the carriage and climbed the rocks on the side, in order to secure some of the beautiful maiden-hair fern which I meant to send by post to my mother in America for her fernery.

Presently an Englishman of athletic build called to me to hand him my trowel, which I did, and he brought me down some beautiful rock ferns which grow only in high places. We walked for a while together, and he told me much about ferns and how they grow where apparently there is no earth.

When we came to the highest point of our journey, he climbed into the big coach and I went back into the carriage. Soon after I was seated Lord A—— said, "You seem to have made an acquaintance outside. You will have to decide whether you will travel with him or with us." I looked at him in mute amazement, as I was not traveling with them, and finally asked, "Why?"

"Because he is an English Jew," he replied.

"I have always been brought up to treat a gentleman as a gentleman, who has treated me as such," I answered.

"It's for you to choose."

"Very well; I will travel with the Jew, then."

After that, neither his lordship nor his daughters spoke to me, and when we reached the Trossachs Hotel for lunch I seated myself next my Jewish benefactor.

He inquired why I had come to his table and, boy fashion, I told him the conversation that had taken place in the carriage.

He said, "They are quite right. I am a Jew. If you would like to travel the rest of the way in the coach with me, I will arrange it."

This he did and told me he was a member of one of the largest manufacturing jewelry concerns in the United Kingdom. When we reached Oban I went to the Great Western Hotel and he to a smaller house.

The next day, Sunday, before my uncle arrived, Mr. J——, the Jew, called on me and said he was leaving for Iverness and gave me a gold scarfpin to remember him by, remarking that he should always remember the American boy who would rather travel with a Jew than an English lord.

Seventeen years passed, and my brother and I were in Pisa, Italy; on taking the train one afternoon for Florence, we found seats in a first-class railway carriage, two seats of which were occupied by two Englishmen.

Before the train started I decided to smoke and (it was the days before corridor cars) I descended to the platform to find a smoking compartment. After I seated myself, I saw that one of the Englishmen from my compartment was entering also. He seated himself near me and began conversation.

"You're an American, aren't you?" he asked.

And when I replied, he said, "I'm from B——."

Immediately my thoughts traveled back to the Trossachs in Scotland, and I said, "I never met but one man from B—— and that was many years ago."

"Who was that?"

"A man named Joseph J——."

"Joseph J——! Where did you meet him?" he inquired.

"Seventeen years ago in the Trossachs of Scotland."

"Oh, then I know your name. Joseph J—— is my youngest brother. He has often told of the American boy who traveled with him to Oban."

The next day we met Mr. J—— and his friend in the Uffizi Gallery and had some conversation with them. They asked if we were going to Rome to attend the Pope's Jubilee and informed us that they had just heard that the hotels had no rooms not already engaged, and that the railway stations were full at night with Spanish priests and other travelers who could not find sleeping accommodations.

As we had not engaged rooms ahead, we hurried to the *poste télégraphe* and sent a message to the Quirinal Hotel, where our father and mother had stayed two years before. Soon we had a reply, "No rooms — better come at once and make reservations."

While dressing early the following morning, as we planned to take the first train for Rome, I received a card from Mr. J—— and on it was written, "Did you secure rooms in Rome?"

I sent word down to him, "We did not. We are going in the early train to Rome. Will be down presently."

When we came downstairs he had gone, but had left an envelope sealed and directed to the Proprietor of the Hotel de Russie at Rome.

We reached Rome and entered the "bus" for Hotel de Russie. When we stopped at the hotel door the porter came out, held up his hands and said, "No rooms. Do not come in." I passed him the envelope from Mr. J——. He read it and beckoned to us to enter. We were given two beautiful rooms with an open fire in the grate of each.

When we inquired how it was possible that they could give us such rooms, the manager, who had accompanied us to the rooms, informed us that Mr. J—— had telegraphed that morning to give us the rooms he and his friend had had engaged for six weeks.

We searched for Mr. J—— and his friend in Rome, but could not find them, and had to satisfy ourselves by writing our thanks and appreciation to this "white" Jew.

The first day at lunch in the Hotel de Russie we sat at one of the five long tables which extended the whole length of the dining salon, the smaller tables having been done away with so as to seat the large number of guests.

Two English ladies whom we had met at Nice two months before were seated opposite. They immediately asked if we were to have those seats permanently, and when told that our names were on the cards at the plates, the older of the two ladies then informed us why she inquired.

"You may be able to solve the mystery of the hotel," she exclaimed. "There will sit beside you to-night at dinner a gentleman who has aroused the curiosity of every woman in the house as to who he is and of what nationality. He speaks to no one."

I smiled and asked, "Do you think I can solve such a mystery, when the ladies have been unable to do it?"

She laughed and said, "Wait until dinner. You will be quite as curious yourself."

That night many of the gentlemen had not dressed for dinner and were wearing cutaway coats, as they were going on to the Corso afterward to see the crowd and hear the music at the Spanish steps. After two courses had been served the seat next to mine was the only one in the dining room which remained unoccupied.

At last the great red curtains at the top of the five steps which led up to the salon were drawn aside and there stood a man six feet or more tall who surveyed the room calmly, looking from table to table. He was very military in his bearing and his clothes fitted him perfectly. His fine features and Vandyke beard attracted the eyes of every one who happened to look to that end of the room.

He descended the steps and walked to the chair next to me. The waiter pushed in his chair, and I heard the gentleman say in Italian, "I'll pass the first courses. Serve me what the others are having now."

In the seats next those occupied by the two English ladies opposite us were two Frenchmen who were in the midst of an animated discussion; one of them leaned across the table and, speaking in French, said that he and his friend differed about something they were discussing and would like to know what the newcomer's opinion was on the subject.

The newcomer smiled and replied in French without any apparent foreign accent that where two people were having an argument he never entered into the controversy and begged to be excused.

The older of the Englishwomen caught my eye and raised her eyebrows as if to say, "This is the man."

Hastily I made up my mind that he was an American or possibly an Englishman.

After a few courses the ladies said they were going to the opera and left the table. My brother said he was going to play billiards with a gentleman and excused himself.

When left alone with the "mystery" I made up my mind to solve the question before I retired.

An offer of salt which was beyond his reach and near my brother's plate opened the conversation.

"You're an American, are you not?" he ventured.

"Yes."

"You and your friend are the only Americans in this hotel. After we finish, will you go to the smoking room with me and answer some questions about your government which I would like to ask?"

"Certainly, it will give me much pleasure," I replied. We were speaking in English and I could not detect the slightest foreign accent, but was convinced from his remark that he was not an American.

When we left the dining room and went into the corridor, he passed me his cigar case and asked me to have a cigar. I can remember that cigar to this day. It was the best one I have ever smoked.

On the corner of the case I observed a crown and a monogram in raised silver. We walked along the corridor to the steps leading down to the lower hall from which the smoking room opened. (This is all changed now and is occupied by the new offices.) When we entered the smoking room the seats were all taken by men and women drinking their coffee and cognac and smoking. We walked to the far end and seated ourselves on a long sofa. He asked me many questions which I knew any Englishman must know about our government, so I stopped believing that he was English.

At last my chance came and I said, "I have answered your questions. Would you mind if I ask you one?"

"No, I will answer any one you wish. What is it?"

"What nationality are you?"

"Oh, my dear fellow, they say that your country is one of all freedom, while mine, they say, is all oppression. I am a St. Petersburg man."

"Really!" I exclaimed. "I have never met a Russian gentleman before."

He asked our names and said he was Chevalier Lopochoff.

"I have been here two weeks," he continued, "and have spoken to no one as they are all Europeans; but you are Americans. You must introduce me to your brother."

At midnight we left the smoking room and he told my brother and me that he drove every morning at eleven o'clock and invited us to drive with him the following morning.

In the smoking room the next day my brother and I stood at the window looking out into the street, and as the horses were so miserable at that period in Rome, we could not help remarking upon the appearance of a fine pair of Arab horses and an open landeau with coachman and footman in the livery of a nobleman's servants on the box. The body of the landeau was painted cream color and black, and the nobleman's coat-of-arms was emblazoned on the side. The coachman and footman had cockades on their tall hats. The whole outfit impressed me immediately with the feeling of grandeur and nobility.

The door of the smoking room opened and the Chevalier entered.

"Oh, Chevalier, look at this pair of horses! They are the finest I have seen in Rome," said I.

"Yes, come on. That is our carriage," he replied, and before we were aware of it he had hurried us to the door of the hotel.

He insisted upon our taking the best seat at the back while he sat opposite.

As we turned from the Piazza del Popolo into the drive ascending the Pincian Hill, I noticed that we were being saluted by all the private carriages; that is, the footman and coachman touched their hats as well as any gentleman in these other pleasure carriages.

"We are being saluted," I remarked to the Chevalier.

"Oh, thanks, I forgot. Will you kindly return it? Then I can get it, too," he said. For an hour, all through the drive, I was lifting my hand to my hat, saluting. It was very wearisome.

On reaching the hotel again, I went into the office to see if tickets for the Pope's Jubilee had arrived which Archbishop Ryan, U. S. A., had promised to send me from the American College, — seats in the Tribune at St. Peter's.

The clerk told me that Mr. Selinsky, the proprietor, wished to speak to me and opened the door of an inner office. Mr. Selinsky came forward and said, "I wished to inquire — did you know the Chevalier before you came here?"

"No, why?" I replied.

"Because he has been here for two weeks and has spoken to no one. Perhaps it is because you are Americans."

"Who is he?" I asked.

"Ah, all we know is that he is registered from St. Petersburg and is said to be the representative of the Czar on the Bulgarian question. He has a retinue with him. The carriage you drove in this morning is sent for him every day, and belongs to the Duke of Tornello, the Mayor of Rome. Come out to the front door." He preceded me to the door and remarked, "You see these two men here walking on the sidewalk? They are in civilian dress, but walk only in front of this hotel. They followed him in a small carriage this morning as they do every day. Every four hours two other men relieve them."

I went to the smoking room where my brother and the Chevalier were. They stood at the billiard table pushing the balls to the cushion at the farther end and seeing which could make the closest return to the cushion in front of them.

"Well, what is the matter?" inquired the Chevalier, without taking his eyes from the ball.

"Matter? What do you mean?" I answered.

"You are different from when you left the carriage. What puzzles you?"

"I was wondering who those two men were who followed us this morning in a small carriage," I said.

"Oh, you observant Americans. I would prefer to explain. The Duke of Tornello is a friend of mine and he sends his carriage for me to use every day, but he has some foolish idea that some Nihilistic trouble might come to me; so he sends these men to watch. All nonsense, but what can I do? Forget it," he laughed and changed the subject.

Two days after he asked me to go with him to a jeweler's on the Corso. He wished to buy a ring for his brother, who was to have a birthday.

At the jeweler's I picked up the most beautiful ring, — a hammered gold band with a diamond, ruby and emerald sunken into the gold.

"Here, send him this," I exclaimed. He immediately seized it and passed it to the jeweler and gave him some instructions and a card upon which an address was evidently written.

"I am so glad you chose that ring. I take

a long time always over a present and it was a great help," he remarked.

The following night after dinner he told me he was going to a musicale at the Duke's palace.

"Come up in my room while I finish dressing." He was in his evening clothes and I could not see that anything was lacking.

"Come on," he cried, as he left the hall and mounted the staircase. There was nothing left for me to do but follow.

When we reached his room and he opened the door, I found we were in a spacious sitting-room and three men in livery jumped to their feet and stood attentive. A secretary came forward and the Chevalier told him to show me the case of photographs while he finished dressing. He disappeared into another room and the secretary gave me a velvet case with pockets in it which contained photographs of wonderful looking women and men, all in court costume. No names were on them.

Presently the Chevalier came back and I saw what his dress had lacked. On his coat were ten decorations, five above and five below. Such crosses I had never seen before, and as I looked at them, one in particular caught my eye. It was of that superb red enamel that has never been produced in modern times outside of Russia

"What is this?" I asked.

"The cross of St. Anne. One has to suffer for Russia before getting that." Then he told me of the hardship he had passed through in the Balkan mountains to win this cross. He showed me the little picture in the center of St. Anne in the fields, with the Czar's monogram in cipher on the reverse side of the cross. The ribbon of red with a yellow edge matched the enamel and gold in color.

We became very good friends and I passed most of the days either driving or walking with the Chevalier. One night he said he was going to the opera.

I sat that evening alone in the smoking room very late. Two men who had been pointed out to me as English M. P.'s came into the room feeling particularly well and happy and called for whisky and soda. They talked very loudly, interrupting my reading. Their conversation at last attracted my attention, as one remarked that Lord Randolph Churchill's visit to Russia was wholly political and had nothing to do with his health, as was reported in the London papers. Then they were very free in saying what the political situations was, and one was most profuse in his explanations to the other M. P.

It was all Dutch to me, but as they had disturbed my reading, I turned to the blank leaves at the back of my book and wrote down what was said. In the morning I showed them to the Chevalier.

"Where did you hear this?" he demanded, and I explained.

"It is most important. Come with me to the *post télégraphe.*" He sent a long telegram to St. Petersburg in cipher.

That evening he said, "You must sit up with me in the smoking room until my despatches come to-night."

"I'll stay up until twelve o'clock, but then to bed," said I. "Not a moment after midnight."

That night he drank a great deal, always champagne.

It was near midnight and we were alone in

the smoking room, sitting before an open fire. The despatches had not arrived. I had drunk all the champagne that was good for me. He sat up and told the waiter to bring another bottle.

"Not any for me. I have had enough," I said.

"Only one more," he persisted.

"No! No more for me," but he ordered another bottle with two glasses.

When the waiter poured out the champagne, the Chevalier took one of the glasses and passed it to me. Then happened a thing which would not have occurred had I not partaken of too much champagne. I took the glass and said, "I told you I would not drink any more and I will not." Thereupon I threw the filled glass into the fire in the grate.

The Chevalier rose without drinking his glass of wine and simply bowing, said "Good night" and left the room.

Angry and chagrined, I took myself to my room and bed and passed an uncomfortable night.

The next morning at eleven o'clock the

secretary of the Chevalier came into the smoking room and said that the Chevalier would like to see me in his room.

Still more angry at myself than at any one else, I replied, "Tell the Chevalier that I am in the smoking room, and if he wants to speak to me he can come here." The man bowed and left the room.

Presently the door flew open and the Chevalier rushed in. With both hands extended, he caught one of my hands and said, "My despatches came at two o'clock this morning and I was able to read them. Everything is all right. Do you know I cannot remember a single thing which occurred last night; can you?"

I assured him that I could not, and we locked arms and walked out into the street, and thus through his tact and diplomacy the episode of the night before was forgotten.

At the beginning of the next week we were leaving in the early afternoon for Naples. We came downstairs to lunch that day at twelve o'clock as our train left at two o'clock.

The head waiter informed us that the

Chevalier was giving us a lunch in the
private dining room and that he had sent
word to a Mr. Carlo, a friend of ours, to lunch
with us. We were soon joined by the others
and sat down to a most enjoyable repast.

When we were about to say good-by
the Chevalier turned to me and said, "Let
your friend go to the station with your
brother, while you come up to my room."

When we entered and he had closed the
door, he took something from his secretary
and passed it to me.

"The first night you came to my room I
remember you admired the cross of St. Anne
of Russia, and while I cannot tell you who
I am, I want you to take this cross to remember me by. We have had a good time together. Some day I will let you know who
I am. I have your address. I am not the
Chevalier Lopochoff and I am not the representative of the Czar on the Bulgarian
question. I have been on a holiday.

"You will hear from me some day; we
both may be old men. You will come to
Russia. You will ask for me. You will
show me this cross and say, 'Roma eighteen

eighty-eight'; and then I will remember. I will show you St. Petersburg."

I took the precious cross in my hand and assured him how much I should prize it and how it would always remind me of him and the glorious time we had had together. We walked to the door of the room, and I inquired if he were coming to the station to see me off. He straightened himself to his full height and answered, "I never go to see any one off. People come to see me depart. Good-by."

Thus we parted after weeks of delightful intimacy. Eight years passed. One day I received a box from the Russian Embassy in Washington. It contained an antique silver casket with a knob of yellow amber on the top. On the underside was engraved

Grand Duke —— ——
Roma 1888.

I have refrained from giving his name as he is still living; to my mind he has proved himself the greatest of all the Romanoff family and to-day is the most popular man among all classes of Russians.

CHAPTER VII

TREASURES FROM ITALY

O N a December morning in Rome, in 1890, there was an account in the newspaper of the uncovering of several marble steps on the Palatine Hill which must have dated back to the time of the Caesars. One of the workmen who was running the dirt through sieves so as to save the small cubes of marble used in the platform of the steps, discovered a translucent irregular stone. After he had washed it, two heads were found carved, — one looking either way. The article in the newspaper said that the stone was found to be a topaz and the cutting probably was Greek.

That day I called at the office of the newspaper and sought for more information on the subject, but all I could learn was that the item of news had been written by some one outside the office and handed in to them for publication. Where the stone could be seen or in whose possession it was they did not know.

The matter passed from my mind. Three months later, in Florence, an Italian friend of mine, also a collector, knowing that I had passed the winter in Rome, asked me if I had heard of the finding of this stone. When he found I was interested he said a friend of his had the stone in Florence and wished to dispose of it. A place was arranged where we were to meet and I was to be shown the gem.

Not feeling sure of my own judgment of an antique of such undoubted value, I begged permission to bring a friend with me. The person I took with me was the best engraver on sardonyx in Florence. The whole meeting had that atmosphere of mystery about it which enhances the charm to the collector.

My engraver produced magnifying glasses with which he made a thorough examination of the herm, as any marble or stone having two heads cut on it is called. Originally the Greeks had these heads cut in marble and mounted on a pedestal when land belonging to two people joined. Each owner's head or portrait was cut facing the piece of land which was his or her property. Many of these dividing stones or herms were beautifully sculptured by the best artists. Soon the sculptors recognized the artistic value of placing the heads in this way instead of simply making busts, and they produced the heads of Greek mythology for decorative purposes in halls and buildings.

My engraver immediately pronounced the two heads as those of Hebe and Hercules, and the stone a topaz. He said the cutting of the features was a lost art, as now a topaz must be cut with facets like a diamond or cabochon ovals; otherwise the stone would chip. When I found that the gem could be purchased, I bought it and brought it to Boston with me.

In the gallery leading from the Persian Gallery to the Greek Room in the Boston Museum of Fine Arts is a small original marble herm with the two faces, Hebe and Hercules, cut exactly like my small gem. It is labeled Greek.

Shortly after this we journeyed to Sienna

on our way to that delightfully situated town of Perugia.

From an Englishman I met in a small hotel in one of the hill towns of Italy I learned that at a castle a few miles away he had picked up a most remarkable tapestry. He said the count who owned the castle was most anxious to dispose of other furnishings in the different rooms. Further explanation disclosed the facts that the Count was a gambler and was selling his belongings quietly to any one so as to get money to pay his debts and give his family food, — and not arouse his heirs to place a guardian over him.

The following week I called at the castle and found the conditions as my acquaintance had stated. Among the furniture offered me were nine dining-room chairs of Spanish-Italian design. They were high back, leather-covered, with turned and carved wooden legs of different designs. The Count said they had belonged to an ancestor of his two hundred and fifty years ago, who was a Cardinal.

He called my attention to one of the nine chairs, the leather of which was different

from the other eight. This particular leather
was tooled in a geometrical design and was
on the Cardinal's own chair. The story was
that in his absence this chair was always
turned face to the wall.

I purchased the chairs, and a carpenter
in the small town near by crated them and
sent them for me to Genoa for shipment
to the United States by the White Star line.

Several months after, I was in Nice in the
south of France, and was notified by the White
Star line in Genoa that the chairs had arrived
there, but that the Italian Government had
seized them as works of art and would not
let them go out of the country. Upon inquiry
I was told that I must have an interview with
the people of the Belle-Arti at Rome.

They informed me that they could not let
these chairs go to America as they did not
have duplicates of them. As I carried photographs of my chairs with me, I asked that one
of their representatives be allowed to accompany me to the Borgia Gallery. In one of the
rooms I produced my photographs of the
chairs and showed him the eight chairs in
this gallery which were exactly like those the

Belle-Arti had held up. He admitted that they were alike, and later the Government released them and they are now on exhibition in Boston.

Two other chairs I found, which date back to the days of the eighteenth century, belonged to Goronwy Owen, the Welsh poet. A number of years ago I was traveling through Wales and at Conway met some charming people who informed me that one of them was the descendant of Owen and invited me to visit his home. There, in the library, were these two chairs which belonged to Wales's greatest poet. I admired them so much that the gentleman said, "If I ever sell them you shall have them."

Only ten years after I received word from a relative of his that he had passed away, but had left the request that I should be allowed to purchase the Owen chairs if I wished. They grace a place in my living room and certainly are distinctly different from any chairs in America.

CHAPTER VIII

OUTWITTING A DEALER

A JEW dealer in antiques in London heard of a pair of chairs made in the reign of William and Mary which had been treasured heirlooms in a family in Sussex.

Previous to 1900 money could not buy these chairs, but that year the owner died and it became a fight between dealers and collectors to possess them.

A friend of mine was going for a visit to Sussex and in the railway carriage leaving London the only other occupant was the London antique-furniture dealer. The Jew was so enthusiastic over the fact that he was to see these chairs that he could not keep it to himself and made a confidant of my friend. They happened to be in the same town my friend was visiting, so when they arrived at the station my friend's curiosity induced him to accept the invitation of the Hebrew to view the chairs, as they were in a house close by the station.

The person who had inherited the treasures pointed out the peculiar construction and the marks of the adze in the cutting of backs and uprights. The Jew immediately began to find fault and disparage the statements and laughed at the price the good woman placed upon the chairs. When she stated that representatives of two of the London museums were coming to see them, the Jew said he would return in the afternoon but could give no such price.

My friend proceeded to the Inn and partook of a luncheon which he did not share with the Jew, who disappeared into the room reserved for the yokels of the town.

After luncheon my friend went back to have another look at the chairs which had fascinated him. He was so impressed with the history the woman gave him of the house and furniture of this old Sussex family that he paid the price she asked and gave her his London address for shipment.

A week later when he returned to London he found a note from the Jew who had pro-

cured his address from the woman. He
accused my friend of "double-crossing" him
and finally ended by offering him a great
advance in the price if he would sell him the
chairs.

My friend wrote, refuting his charge that
he had double-crossed him, and told him that
his treatment of the gentlewoman who had
so kindly shown them the chairs induced
him to return and purchase them at her price,
— afterwards finding what a prize he had
made; also that they had been sold to a
collector in Boston and shipped.

For fifteen years these chairs have been
exhibited in the Museum of Fine Arts.

CHAPTER IX

IN QUEST OF SYRIAN CHESTS

TWENTY years ago my wife and I were visiting an artist in New York in one of the most artistic and delightful houses in old New York on Tenth Street. My friend took me into the storeroom on the floor with the studio in the upper story of the house and showed me things which he had collected in the East many years before.

Among other things were the carved fronts of old Syrian chests or dower chests. The chests themselves had been destroyed and only the carved fronts kept. They were carved in ironwood and were so old they resembled stone more than wood. The pattern was Byzantine in design and many were inlaid with mother-of-pearl and silver.

I was so charmed with the motive of the design and the almost crude use of the wood-carver's tools that I fear I manifested more interest in them than I should. However, my artist friend did not forget it, and at Christmas time I was the recipient of one of those most beautiful chest fronts.

This art has passed in Syria and fine carving and inlaying is now poorly imitated in coarse reproductions.

When later I had a chest made of birch, which had been so exposed to the weather and sun as to take on the color of the old panel of ironwood, and the carved front was inserted, the chest called forth the admiration of all my friends.

One of the failings of the amateur collector is that when he possesses one specimen he craves more of the same kind; this is where my family declare the danger lies, for possession creates an appetite which is not satisfied with a duplicate but many more. How well I know this to be true, although I would not admit it to the members of my family who are as much interested in the exchequer as I am myself.

On a Sunday afternoon several months after coming into possession of this chest, I wandered into the Boston Public Library and up to the open shelves and looked for a book to while away the time. The kind Providence which I believe looks after the amateur collector — although some of my family think it is not kind Providence but a double horned gentleman with a tail; but whoever it was — guided me to a book entitled "Romance in Syria."

I sat down to peruse it and became immediately interested. It was written by an Englishwoman fifteen years before. It told of a young Presbyterian going out from England as a missionary to Syria. He established himself in a mountain town, opened a school, and men and boys and grown women and girls attended. One most attractive young Syrian woman seemed brighter and more anxious to learn than the others. Soon the young man found he was in love with her. When he spoke to her she said she did not love him, and even if she did she could not marry him as he was a Christian and she was a Mohammedan.

Shortly her brother with whom she lived was taken very ill, and the native doctor, after several visits, gave him up and said

he would die, and that he would not visit
him again. The missionary learned that in
the old days when a man was given up by
the doctor, all his men friends deserted him
and left him to die. The sister was nearly
distracted, as he was her only relative.
The young Englishman then came forward
and ministered unto him, and with European
medicines brought him through to recovery.
The young girl was most grateful, and from
that time recognized the fact that the Christian religion held something that was not
in the teachings of her religion, and soon,
with her brother, became a convert. Shortly
she became engaged to the teacher, and her
brother, being very poor, said he had nothing
he could give her except the old dower chest
which had been handed down in the family
for many years.

At the bottom of the page was a footnote
saying, "These chests may still be found
in the houses in the mountain towns of Syria."

That set me off. Here I had a clew to more
chests like the ones my friend had brought
from Damascus twenty years before. I took
from the book the name of the mountain

town mentioned in the "Romance," and wrote the next day to the Secretary of the Presbyterian Mission, enclosing a photograph of my chest, and inquired if such chests might be picked up at this time. Months went by. I was beginning to realize what a fool thing it was to expect a reply when I received a letter from an Irishman who had a school near the Syrian town. He wrote that there was no Presbyterian school in that town and the authorities in the post-office had given him my letter for translation. He said that as soon as they heard it read, they gave up all interest in it, but that he himself was so pleased to see a letter written in English, for he had been out there fourteen years and his family had lost all interest in him and had ceased to write him, and would I as a favor to him continue to write him every other month. It would seem so good to read English.

Regarding the chests, he had shown the photograph to a number of his converts, and they said they knew where they could get them; so if I would send him a draft for so much money on the Bank of Smyrna, he would have them collect the chests and send them to me. I was overjoyed. I had found a well which had never been tapped and which might bring forth many treasures.

That afternoon I went to York Harbor to pass the week end with my family, and after dinner in the evening I gathered them about me and read the Irishman's letter from Syria. I had expected to hear an outburst of joy such as I felt in my manly breast when they had heard it through; nothing of the sort occurred. Instead, in those quiet tones which my better half can use to tone down my enthusiasm she asked, "You certainly do not intend to send this utter stranger money for more chests when we" (pointing to the daughters) "need so many things?" How quickly an enthusiastic amateur collector can cool off. Under such conditions there is nothing to say. Before I returned to Boston on Monday morning the family wanted me to promise that I would not send that man a draft on the Bank of Smyrna. While I did not actually promise, I said enough (which had been acquired by long practice on other occasions) to allay their fears and yet leave open a hole for me to crawl out of without becoming an actual Ananias.

After a few days in Boston the spell came over me again and I could not resist the temptation of gambling on my belief in the man in Syria. Consequently Kidder, Peabody and Company drew me a draft on the Bank of Smyrna for a number of hundred dollars and I sent it to the Irishman. I can assure you, kind reader, that I did not let the family know about it.

Months went by and no acknowledgment came from Syria, — and I grew stronger each week in the determination that I would guard my secret more closely than ever.

One day — I shall never forget with what delight I seized a great blue envelope with big red seals on the back and Turkish stamps on the front and tore it open. There was a letter from my correspondent, saying he had received the draft and that his scholars had been some time picking up the old Syrian chests. He enclosed a large, long, blue-paper document, with more red seals and a blue ribbon, which he said was a sworn statement that all the chests were over one hundred years old, so that I could escape paying duties. I opened it and did not doubt his word, but the whole thing was written in Turkish.

The chests would have taken up so much room in shipping, they had been knocked asunder, since they were dovetailed together at the corners, and then roped together and each bundle bound in burlap with the carvings and inlays face to face in the center. There were six bundles. When he said in his letter that he had put them on the backs of three donkeys and sent them one hundred and twenty miles across the mountains to Beirut on the sea to be shipped to me at Alexandria, I could not believe he had made such a blunder. However, I consulted the Cunard Line people, and they instructed me to write to the Allendale Line at Alexandria to seize anything marked with my name and send it to their line in Liverpool and they would forward them to Boston.

Seven more months went by; then the Customhouse in Boston notified me of their arrival. When I found the six great rolls of heavy boards done up in burlap, which was torn and dirty, I said to the Customhouse people, "These chests are over one hundred years old; in fact, very much older; they come in free and pay no tax of duty."

"How do we know?" inquired a son of Erin.

"This will certify that my statement is true," I replied, handing him the blue document written in Turkish.

He looked at it and took a side glance at me.

"Do you suppose any of us can read that stuff?" he remarked.

"I thought you might, as this place seems to be filled with Turks," I said, but he did not appreciate my humor.

"You'll have to pay thirty-five per cent duty on the value, according to the invoice."

I answered I never would and left in a huff.

The next morning while reading my paper on the way to town I saw an item from the Associated Press that cholera had broken out in the mountain towns of Syria and was killing many each day. Armed with this paper, I proceeded to the Customhouse and again encountered the man at the desk where the bundles of wood were on one side.

"So you've decided to pay the duty," he chuckled.

"No," said I, "but I saw this in the paper this morning and that's where these chests came from."

He took the paper and read it.

"Look here, I'll give you just an hour to get those things out of here," he cried with apparent alarm.

"How about the duty?" I asked.

"D—— the duty. You get them away."

In an hour they were safe in an unoccupied store of mine, being fumigated.

The following days a carpenter and a cabinetmaker put the chests together, as the separate pieces were all numbered with chalk. In all there were twelve chests. I was astonished. Some fronts were all carved, some were carved and inlaid with mother-of-pearl and silver. The old hinges and locks were of great antiquity. In putting them together the ironwood was so hard it was impossible to drive a nail into it.

The design is conventional Arabic with two, three, four or five trees inlaid or carved. The number of trees show with which wife the chest came to the family. One large chest has four everlasting trees inlaid with mother-of-pearl and silver, designating that it came with the fourth wife.

These are all three or four hundred years old, and the old ones are difficult to acquire. Four of these are in the Museum of Fine Arts in Boston.

Some years or more after receiving these chests, my Irishman wrote that he had been working as an engineer where some trestle ironwork had to be supported over a stream by being built on solid rock foundation. They had uncovered thirty feet below the surface and believed that they had found rock beneath. Upon further excavating, a twelfth-century small town was uncovered. The buildings of stone and cement were encased in mud and rubbled stone, but many of the rooms in the houses were free from débris and one could walk through them. The workmen brought out forty-seven pieces, all whole, of old Roman and Syrian glass, mostly toilet articles and small vases. The surface of these vessels had been attacked by the gases and dampness, and the metal, such as copper and lead used in the manufacture of the glass, had come to the surface in the disintegration and had taken on the most beautiful iridescent colors, with a pearl-like substance for the background. My friend wrote that he had taken possession of them all, and if I wanted them, to cable him, care of the Bank of Smyrna, which I did. Most of these pieces are now in a glass case in the Persian Room of the Museum in Boston.

Then the war came on, and as I was in Europe just before that, I wrote my friend in Syria about more carvings, but he replied that he was returning with his family to Ireland and gave no address.

Three years passed. A letter came to me from Syria. Yes, it was from my friend, again in Damascus. He wrote me of the conditions there and that he had left his family in Ireland and only returned to Syria to look after his personal belongings. He begged me not to answer his letter, as misinterpretation might be put on anything I might write and make it dangerous for him.

I received that letter in December, 1916. The following month I read in the paper that

English teachers and others in Syria had been seized and thrown into prison. Fearing for my correspondent and knowing that our United States Embassy at Constantinople had taken over the British affairs, I wrote to Washington and gave my friend's name and asked them at my expense to find him and if in prison to use every endeavor to free him. The Washington Office of State immediately wrote that they had cabled our ambassador at Constantinople and as soon as anything was heard from him I should be advised.

Two months went by before I received word that my friend had been found, with a friend, in prison and had been taken to Beirut and put on one of our American ships for Smyrna, where he would find an English ship and would be safe.

In 1920 another letter came from Syria; once again he had returned, this time with the British Relief Association. He wrote me of the great suffering of the poor in Damascus. In finishing his letter he said, "A strange occurrence when I was in Damascus, — one of your government representatives intervened in my behalf, and a friend and I were freed and taken to Beirut. The last thing I saw as we steamed away was your United States representative waving a small American flag."

Thereupon I mailed him the Washington correspondence and feel that I have partly paid my debt to the man who collected my chests and glass.

SYRIAN CHESTS CARVED AND INLAID

Seventeenth Century

Boston Museum of Fine Arts, George Blake Dexter Collection

CHAPTER X

THE MANDARIN'S GIFT

A DOCTOR in Tien-Tsin, China, sent me a box of curios and asked me to look them over and he would make a price on any of them I desired.

There was a string of beautiful blue beads which looked to me like those I had seen in the Persian collections in London. Those in the European museums contain twenty-six or less beads; this string has just a hundred. Each bead was like turquoise matrix. They were Persian enamels.

My friend the doctor wrote that he was sent for to diagnose the case of a mandarin in Pekin who was very ill. He hurriedly left Tien-Tsin and reached Pekin, to find the man still alive, but suffering great pain. He ordered everything to be prepared for an immediate operation for appendicitis.

The old man was lying in a bed of red

lacquer, and instead of a mattress the body of the bed was stone and covered with bear and wolf skins lined with silk. Under the stone, which rested on its four corners on stone feet, was space enough to build a fire of wood on the stone floor to keep the bed warm. This is considered one of the greatest of luxuries.

The patient did not seem to mind the thought of the operation but inquired of the doctor, "How long before the fever will leave me after the operation is over?"

"Two days."

"How soon will I be up on my feet?" the mandarin inquired.

"Two weeks, if you have no drawback."

"You will stay that two weeks?" he almost demanded.

"Oh, no, I must return to Tien-Tsin in two days."

"You will stay for two weeks. We will now have the operation."

It passed off successfully. At the end of two days the fever was gone; the doctor prepared for his departure.

The mandarin, knowing the foreigner's curiosity and this particular one's love for the beautiful antique said (noticing the preparations for leaving):

"To-morrow when the sun draws behind its purple cloud at the end of the day, the major-domo will open the black lacquer chest in the hall. It is only opened twice a year."

"But I will not be here," the doctor said.

"You will stay and see the collection of carved crystals and jade in the chest. Many people would travel many moons to look upon this collection," he went on.

The consequence was that the doctor stayed, and each day the wily old Chinaman had some new device to keep the doctor on and prevent his leaving Pekin. The days passed and as they approached the two weeks' limit, the doctor made up his mind that no scheme on the part of his old patient would induce him to stay the two weeks, so he planned to go the day before the two weeks were completed.

In the late afternoon of that day, he went into the room in which the old man sat.

"I am going to-night and I want to bid

you good-by and assure you how pleased I am to leave you so well."

The skinny long fingers of the mandarin supported his head as his elbows rested on his knees. His eyes were closed, and he muttered as if to himself.

"The great steel-encased cabinet works by ancient clockwork. To-morrow the floor in the main hall will slide open and this cabinet, which contains the priceless Persian enamels, will appear and I myself will show you a string of beads that came from Tibet — and are one thousand years old."

"I cannot remain even to see these wonderful enamels," answered the doctor, struggling with himself to strangle the curiosity arising in his breast.

Without paying any attention to the doctor's remark, the old fellow continued his dissertation:

"This string of enamels has been the source of controversies between princes and the great ones of the East. Princesses have been offered in exchange for these one hundred beads. You must see them."

Alas! the doctor's courage was failing him,

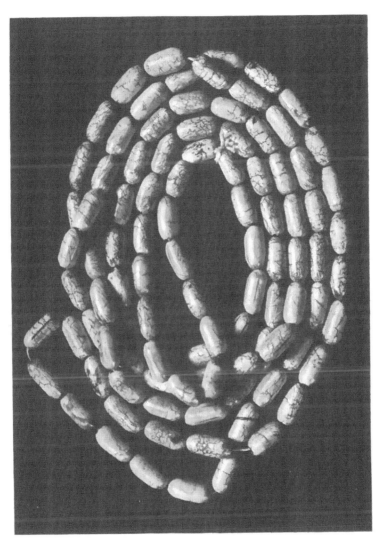

PERSIAN ENAMEL BEADS
Eleventh Century
ONE SIXTH ORIGINAL SIZE

and he wrote that with one extreme exertion he arose and explained that nothing could detain him longer.

The Chinaman smiled and replied, "You will remain without force, because I am very grateful to you for saving my life. No money can repay you, but down deep in your heart is a love for the beautiful, and to express to you my appreciation of your friendship and your skill I am going to give you this string of Persian enamels."

The doctor's firmness gave way and he remained.

The next morning the clockwork opened the floor in the great hall and then slowly, as if raised by invisible hands, a wonderful carved cabinet was disclosed as the outer steel shell unfolded itself and sunk back into the opening in the floor. When the cabinet stood alone, the old mandarin unlocked its door with a curious old enamelled key, and an inner small cabinet disclosed two small drawers divided by a partition. The drawers he drew out, then the partition came forward and uncovered a small hole only large enough to put a match in. Pressing the match against a spring, the secret chamber became apparent. A small box was taken out and there, lying in lamb's wool, was the Persian enamel string of beads.

So the beads were sent to me to dispose of, but I could not let them go. Some things are too beautiful and wonderful to sell. We arrived at a price by which I could possess them.

To own some one thing that has no duplicate in the world, made by an artist who put his soul and all his love into this object, the pride of his life, the product of his own thought! On such there is no money value! The miser may hoard his money. What is it after all, — so much silver and gold. Any man can work and accumulate money; but where is the man with another string of Persian enamel beads?

CHAPTER XI

THE LEGEND OF THE DOWER CHEST

ON a Sunday morning in the spring of 1905, while walking on a street in Florence, Italy, I noticed a man standing in a doorway of a house. As I approached him he said, "Will you come in and see some fine old Italian furniture?"

At first I hesitated, but my curiosity overcame my better judgment and I entered. On the street floor there was a large assortment of odds and ends which had the appearance of being recently acquired and to which the owner paid no attention. He mounted the staircase at the back of the hall and waited for me to follow, for I had stopped to examine a chest of drawers near the foot of the stairs. The drawers were bespattered with mud which had dried on to the surface of the front.

On the floor above there were many beautiful pieces of old furniture, but they had all been restored and newly polished and robbed of the antique effect so dear to a collector's heart. With the exception of two chairs, I found that there was nothing which I cared to purchase.

When we retraced our steps and were again in the lower hall, I inquired about the chest of drawers.

"Oh, that is not a chest of drawers; it is a desk," remarked the dealer.

In the meantime I had dampened my handkerchief and rubbed away some of the mud, disclosing the beautiful Italian walnut. On the top of the desk was a large key which unlocked it; half of the slab on the top folded back and the front of one of the supposed drawers fell forward, held by quaint chains. Inside were ten small drawers of olive wood quaintly fashioned and beveled. Inside one of these small drawers was a string which opened up a secret drawer. I asked where the piece came from. The dealer said his agent had found it in an old castle near Genoa.

"What will you sell it for?" I inquired.

ITALIAN DESK
Seventeenth Century
Boston Museum of Fine Arts, George Blake Dexter Collection

"I cannot tell what it will cost to restore it," he answered.

"Oh, I want it just as it is, mud and all," I replied.

We soon came to a price, including crating and delivery to the White Star line at Genoa.

I had been at home in Boston two months before it arrived.

After it was thoroughly washed and rubbed with olive oil, I found it was a genuine sixteenth-century piece. All the front is beautifully put together in blocks of walnut, so warping could never take place. The moldings are beautiful examples of handwork. The handles, of exquisitely carved bronze, are gems of the metal-worker's art. For many years it has stood in the large Italian Room in the Museum of Fine Arts in Boston.

Next to it is a dower chest of apple wood inlaid on the top and sides with crests of many families related to the Spanish Royal House of the seventeenth century. The Dutch inlays at that time were very beautiful and were only executed for noble families. The different colors were produced by the use of different woods. Tulip wood, placed in hot sand and baked, produced a pinkish color that will never fade. The brown inlay was pear wood, treated in the same way. The green was tulip wood baked in hot sand between layers of mulberry leaves, thus extracting the green and dyeing the wood, which has lasted three hundred years without fading.

This chest was picked up in a stable near Marlboro, Massachusetts, and at the time was divided by a board in the center and used for grain and blankets. The foreigner who had it would not say where he procured it, but was quite willing to part with it.

In the long corridor on the lower floor of the Evans Memorial addition to the Museum of Fine Arts, Boston, is a black oak Flemish chest which takes four men to lift it. This has a carved front of period design and in the carving the name, "Lanke Toden A.D. 1692." For many years this chest had been in the great hall of one of the famous castles in England. The ladies, who are the last of their family, were living in the castle in 1916; they intimated to a friend of mine that they wished to sell some of the furnishings, as their taxes and expenses had made

DUTCH INLAID CHEST
Seventeenth Century
Boston Museum of Fine Arts, George Blake Dexter Collection

such inroads on their income there was no other alternative.

Among other furniture was this oak chest. Photographs were taken of it and sent to me. Then the chest came to Boston. The legend which accompanied it was as follows:

In the year 1692, two years after William of Orange came to England, the owner of the castle decided to have a set of tapestries made in Flanders for the great hall walls. A young man, Lanke Toden, an artist, was sent from Flanders to take measurements and to talk over the designs required.

One of the subjects chosen was Diana of the Chase. The great forest which at that time surrounded the castle aroused the young artist's admiration and he made many sketches of the woods. One day he saw two stags in deadly combat with their antlers linked together. It gave him an inspiration, and he made sketches of Diana with her women attendants passing through the wood and confronted by many stags in combat, with their antlers linked, forming a complete barrier to the advancing Diana. Following the story of the goddess of hunting who

abjured marriage, the artist introduced a
spirit form of a knight, armed with spear
and shield, to protect her and her fair fol-
lowers.

While at work on the painting, which was
to be submitted to the lord of the castle before it was sent to Flanders to be reproduced
in tapestry, he learned that there was a fair
daughter of the castle whom he had not seen
and who was most carefully guarded. To
study the wood as a background for his
picture, he rose very early one morning and
entered the forest. In a clearing he suddenly
came across a young maiden who was trying
to extricate herself from an entanglement of
vines and bushes. When she saw him she
became greatly confused, and on his releasing
her from the vines, she fled to the castle. He
had seen enough to impress upon his mind
her fair beauty, and her startled expression
was what he sought for his tapestry for the
face of Diana. He found his canvas and at
once painted in the face as he remembered it.

For weeks, knowing the lovely maiden was
zealously guarded, he sought her, until he
became aware that she was seeking him also,

and their clandestine meetings in the early morning were occurring so frequently that the artist became alarmed. Boldness was his virtue, however, and he immediately proceeded to paint his own features into the face of the spirit knight. When one day the owner of the castle insisted upon seeing the painting, he recognized the portraits of his daughter and the spirit knight. He was very wroth. His ambition for his daughter was much higher than to marry her to an artist and a foreigner. The maiden's mother was appealed to by the young people, but she said she would never be willing that her daughter should leave England and go to Flanders to live; whereupon the young artist replied that Art could live anywhere and he would give up Flanders and swear allegiance to the English throne so long as he could rescue Diana from the barrier which confronted her.

All went well and his father was well pleased with his son's decision. For his wedding gift he sent the dower chest with his son's name carved into the wood and the date, — 1692 — Lanke Toden.

In the Lawrence Room in the Boston Museum of Fine Arts is a chest of drawers of black oak made in the seventeenth century, probably one of the best Jacobean examples in this country. Many years ago it stood in Newstead Abbey, which then belonged to Lord Byron's family. Long after Lord Byron had sold the Abbey to Colonel Wildman the furniture was retained.

In 1828 Sir Richard Phillips in his "Personal Tour" writes:

"Night overtaking me at Newstead Abbey, the splendid hospitality of Colonel Wildman was kindly exerted, and he indulged a sentimental traveller by allowing me to sleep in Byron's bed in Byron's room."

When in later years the Abbey ownership again changed, the furniture of the older part of the Abbey was sold. A family in Mansfield, a few miles away, procured the Jacobean chest and I purchased it from them some thirty years ago.

In a drawer which would not close tightly I found wedged a book of letters of John Hughes, the author of the great drama of the "Siege of Damascus," which in 1719 held

FLEMISH CHEST, DATE 1692
Boston Museum of Fine Arts, George Blake Dexter Collection

the stage in London. Mrs. M. Porter, the great actress, acted the part of Eudocia. In the book is a letter from this excellent actress and under the letter, written in pencil, is reference to an account written in ink upon the last flyleaf of the book, giving the reason why this popular actress was lost to the stage in 1730.

It reads as follows:

"Mrs. Porter, the actress, lived at Highwood Hill near Hendon; after the play she went home in a one-horse chaise; her constant companions were a book and a brace of horse pistols. In the summer of 1731, as she was taking the air in her chaise, she was stopped by a highwayman who demanded her money. She had the courage to present one of her pistols to him; the man who perhaps had only with him the appearance of firearms, assured her that he was no common thief, that robbing on the highway was not to him a matter of choice but necessity, and in order to relieve the wants of his poor distressed family; he informed her at the same time where he lived and told her such a melancholy story that she gave him all the money in her purse which was about ten guineas.

"The man left her; upon this she gave a lash to the horse, he suddenly started out of the track and the chaise was overthrown, this occasioned the dislocation of her thighbone. Let it be remembered to her honor that not withstanding this unlucky and painful accident, she made strict inquiry after the robber and finding that he had not deceived her, she raised amongst her acquaintances about £60 which she took care to send him.

"Such an action in a person of high rank would have been celebrated as something great and heroic; the feeling mind will make no distinction between the generosity of an actress and that of a princess."

Who wrote this I know not, but it was written before Lord Byron was born, and the book must have been in the Abbey in the old chest of drawers during his life at Newstead.

CHAPTER XII

REASSEMBLING THE FAMILY
PLATE

IN the year 1756 Richard Dexter married
Rebecca Peabody of Salem and Boxford.
Her father had a house in each place. The
Boxford house was standing until within a
few years; then it was destroyed by fire.
When Rebecca Peabody married, her father
sent to London for a tea service and a coffee
set made of the then new Sheffield Plate which
had first appeared in 1750. This was Rebecca
Peabody's wedding gift. She later acquired
other pieces to the number of thirteen.

In the following one hundred and fifty
years these different pieces of Sheffield Plate
had become separated from each other and
were in many different hands, but mostly in
possession of the direct descendants.

About fifty years ago my father received
a letter from an antique dealer in Newbury-

port, saying he had four pieces of a coffee
set of silver on copper marked

Rebecca Peabody Dexter
1756

He stated that it was much the worse for
wear and he would sell the four pieces cheap.
As it did not interest my father, my grandmother gave me money and told me (a boy)
that they had belonged to an ancestor of
mine and to go to Newburyport and purchase
them. Full well do I remember taking a
carpetbag and going from Boston to Newburyport in search of this treasure. I was
not to tell the man my name or seem particularly interested in the coffee set, —
these were the instructions of my grandmother.

Entering the shop, I looked at many things
and priced them. At last in an old desk, with
bookcase above it, I noticed the tarnished set
of four pieces, a coffee pot, a hot-water pot,
sugar and creamer. They were dented and
twisted, but I could see the name and date
engraved upon them. This held me.

"What are these?" I inquired.

JACOBEAN CHEST
Sixteenth Century
Boston Museum of Fine Arts, George Blake Dexter Collection

The old man unlocked the bookcase and took the four pieces out.

"You see how they're marked. I have written all the Dexters in Boston, but I guess they don't care for them. All those roses and flowers around the edge are solid silver. They were fine pieces in their day. You can have them for twenty dollars."

After hesitating and seeming to lose interest in the pieces, I said that I would take them. Soon afterward I returned to Boston with my treasure.

Taking them to one of the large silver and jewelry houses the next day, I found that the price for restoring them would be so great that I put them back in the carpetbag and walked away.

I had not gone more than a block when I was overtaken by a boy about my own age, who said:

"I works up in that store you were just in, and I heard what the man told you it would cost to fix those pieces up. Don't you let on, but I'll show you where the man's place is who does it for them, and he'll do it for you cheap."

We walked down Washington Street to Harvard Place opposite the Old South Church, and in a tumble-down building we went up rickety stairs. Then the boy pointed to a door and said, "Now I'll go, but don't you give me away."

The little old Englishman, silver plater and general mender of all things silver, looked at the set of Sheffield Plate.

"Beautiful! Fine!" he cried. "I shall love to restore them as good as they ever were. How much? Oh, a five-dollar bill will put them in perfect shape."

So I left them and in a week's time they were sent home and all the relatives came to see them. This opened up the subject, and I heard from one distant relative after another that they had a single piece belonging to the original thirteen pieces. A gentleman in New York wrote me that he had four pieces and would leave them to me when he died; that was not very promising, — although ten years afterward he made the long journey and his father wrote me that in their house in New York he had found a box marked for me and was sending it to me.

This box contained four more pieces, three of a small tea set, and a wine cooler.

Some years after a man from Lynn, Massachusetts, came to see me. His name was W—— and an ancestor of his had married into the Dexter family. He was over seventy years of age and told me that in his attic was an old silver platter with a larger stand under it. When he was a boy his brother and he had played cooking with it, as there were two copper lamps underneath the platter. I became deeply interested. Then I thought I was being taken in, for he told me of his extreme poverty and asked if I had any clothing I could give him. Not to be daunted, I said I would send him some clothes if he would send me the old platter with the lamps, etc. After he had left me, I immediately lived up to my end of the bargain and despatched a suit and overcoat I could not use again, and, true to his word, and better, a box arrived with not only the platter, lamps and stand, but an oval cover with a wonderful solid silver handle on the top. The platter was large enough to take a fourteen-pound turkey, the lamps large enough to keep him hot, and the cover large enough to cover the bird when on the platter. This was the crowning piece of the thirteen.

In another branch of the family the candlesticks twenty inches high turned up, and a kind Providence removed the good old lady who possessed them and who designated that they should join the group; so they came to me.

What the other pieces were we could only surmise.

Years went by and then a gentleman in Salem wrote me that in his branch of the Endicott family they had a hot-water urn with a coat-of-arms engraved on it that was not theirs, and would I go down to Salem and look at it.

The next day found me in Salem. The urn stands thirty inches high and is most beautifully modelled. On the front was finely engraved the coat-of-arms and crest of the Dexter family. We traced how it came to them through a branch of the Peabody family, and now it too is added to the original set.

A curious way of keeping the water hot in the urn is shown when the top is removed.

A tube of silver supported by a framework is opened by unscrewing a round cover. Inside is a ten-inch-long iron window weight, with a hole in the top through which a poker can be thrust. Thus the iron window weight was removed, placed in the coals of a grate until red hot, then replaced in the tube. When the urn is filled with hot water and the red-hot window weight is put into the tube, and the top of the tube screwed on, it will keep the water hot for three hours.

I despaired of ever tracing the other two pieces of the thirteen, when an utter stranger wrote me she had the two covered dishes which belonged to the set and would part with them for a consideration. She knew her business and also how much I wanted them. She thought she got the best of the bargain, — but I doubt it. There are things that are beyond price.

CHAPTER XIII

THE RESULT OF MISTAKEN IDENTITY

ON the twentieth of October, 1905, an American friend of mine was at his tailor's in High Holborn, just finishing a trying-on, when an English acquaintance, a Londoner, rushed into the tailor's shop and said, "I'm jolly glad to find you. The woman at your lodgings said you were here. Now be lively and come with me to Sir Henry Irving's funeral at the Abbey. You'll always regret it if you miss it."

"That's all very well, but I can't go in this gray suit," my friend answered.

The tailor came to the rescue and produced a pair of black trousers, saying, "You pull these on over your gray trousers and I'll take up the extra width in the back of the waist with a large safety pin." "After that," my friend added, "I felt quite secure and that

I was not apt to fall to pieces; the tailor offered his black overcoat which fitted me fairly
well.   The tailor's assistant put a piece
of crepe around my hat.   We were just ready
to start, when I spoke of not having any
black gloves.   My friend said he had a pair
and offered me the right and kept the left-hand
one for himself.   Our other hands went into
our pockets.   Soon we were in a four-wheeler
bound for Westminster Abbey.

"The crowd outside was seeking admission
at the small door.   My friend, who is most
impetuous if once started, saw that a few
people were entering the large door, and
grabbing me by the arm cried out, 'Here
you are; this is your place,' and pushed me
in through the large door — and strange to
say we found ourselves inside the Abbey.

"We kept close to those ahead of us, and
not until we had advanced halfway up the
aisle did we realize that we were in the pro-
cession of family mourners.   There was no
such thing as turning back; so we proceeded
to seats in the second front row."

My friend said that on coming to the back
of the Abbey, where he and his friend hoped

to drop out, one of the men mourners moved close to him and whispered, "I know how fond you were of Sir Henry and he of you; so I want you to take this as a remembrance of him," and pressed a small package into my friend's hand. He was so dumbfounded at being evidently taken for some intimate friend of the great actor that he could make no reply.

My friend and the Londoner slipped out of the Abbey into the crowd and took a cab back to the tailor's to divest themselves of their borrowed weeds.

When he opened the package which had been passed to him in the Abbey, he found a souvenir from William II to Henry Irving in appreciation of his talent as an actor.

The next day this souvenir pin was returned through the proper channel with an explanation that it was bestowed on the wrong person. What a chance for an amateur collector!

CHAPTER XIV

THE WAITER'S SNUFFBOX

THIRTY years ago in Soho, London, there was a famous Italian restaurant to which many people went nightly, as they could order real Italian dishes, and spaghetti was cooked in true Neapolitan style, better than at any other place in London.

My friend and I went there repeatedly and sat at a table in a far-off corner where we could see all that went on in the other parts of the room.

From the first night the Italian who waited upon us attracted our attention; his style and general appearance were in direct contrast with the other attendants; he was always courteous and interested in our ordering and often suggested special Italian dishes. The dinner ended, we usually settled ourselves back in the corner to listen to the music of a Venetian band of singers. The first night our waiter approached to offer us a light from wax taper matches which he took from a curious |matchsafe which looked more like a snuffbox than anything else. The second night I put out my hand for the box when he produced the matches. On examination, what I thought was carved wood proved to be amber.

"This is amber," I remarked to the waiter.

"Yes," he answered. "Old Sicilian, two hundred years old."

On one side is the portrait medallion of some war chief of other days and on the other side is a figure of a helmeted soldier with the flags and implements of war. The ends and borders are beautifully cut in a floral design.

Finally our last dinner at this famous restaurant was ended and we bade Geronimo, the waiter, farewell. He smiled as we left him and quietly said, "I hope we may meet again sometime, perhaps under different circumstances."

My friend often referred to this curious parting.

Three years later I was in Naples. I had been asked by an architect, before leaving

America, to carry with me a Persian tile which he desired to have reproduced by Sabota, the Neapolitan tile maker.

On the second day in Naples I took the tile and the slip of paper with the address of Sabota and journeyed forth, believing it to be a very simple task to locate Sabota and his tile works. Did you, dear reader, ever try to find a shop from an address in the old part of Naples?

In the lower town I made inquiry from two strangers who were immediately joined by two others. They conversed in Italian and then the last two said they would conduct me to the house of Sabota. We passed through many streets and out of the lower town into streets that were narrower and where the buildings were taller. We met fewer people. Several times I hesitated, but they reassured me and presently we stood before a sinister-looking doorway.

Until that moment I had not noticed that we were being followed. One of my guides opened the door of the house and beckoned to me, while the other held up four fingers to indicate the fourth floor.

A voice behind us said, "Don't go in there," and then like a wild beast he cursed and raved at my guides, who shrank back from the doorway; upon a further tirade they fled.

"You should not be here," he remarked. "What are you in search of?"

I produced the paper with the address of Sabota. He read it and shook his head.

"You were either going to be robbed or blackmailed. Either is bad enough in Naples."

We turned and walked back to the lower town and soon found Sabota's shop.

My deliverer waited until I had completed my mission. As we walked to my hotel, I thanked him for his great kindness. He smiled, passing me a box of cigarettes, and as he put the box in his pocket, he said, "Let me give you a light," and thereupon produced the Sicilian snuffbox I had seen in Soho. I gasped and looked into his face. It was Geronimo, the waiter.

"Geronimo," I cried.

"Yes, but not a waiter," he laughingly answered. "I am an officer in the Navy. I was hard pushed for money when you met me three years ago in London. The position

INTAGLIO
Actaeon and Hounds, with impression in wax

TOPAZ HERM
Heads of Hercules and Hebe

SICILIAN SNUFF BOX

of waiter was the only thing I could get to do. It was a great experience."

He dined with me that night, and two evenings later I dined at the house of his brother, Baron B——. My visit to Naples was a delight and I had the entrée to many private galleries and saw things from a different stand, all because of the snuffbox, — which is now in my possession.

CHAPTER XV

CHINESE PORCELAINS

AT the time of the outbreak of the Great War, the German consul in one of the larger cities of China, after a residence of twenty-six years, was obliged to make a hurried exit from his post and return to the Fatherland.

The consul had devoted himself for many years to collecting old Chinese porcelains. Among his many pieces was a "hawthorn jar" in blue and white. The jar stands twenty-eight inches high and is the duplicate of one in the British Museum which some years ago was found in an obscure shop in London, and bought for five pounds sterling; afterward this jar brought $2700 in a sale in London and was then given to the British Museum.

This duplicate was sent to the United States by an agent of the German consul and was minus the teakwood cover and stand and therefore lost its artistic attractiveness.

Fortunately I was familiar with its dupli-cate in London and recognized its worth and purchased it for a trifle. In a subsequent shipment to Boston of other pieces of this collection, a teakwood cover and stand were offered for sale, but in this last shipment there was no jar they would fit, and they were sacrificed, as no one wanted them but myself. Imagine my joy, upon taking them home, to find they were the missing pieces for the jar I had bought months before.

The blue background of the jar representing the broken ice with the prune flowers in white typifies the coming of spring to the Chinese mind.

Among a number of household goods sent from a Toronto home to be sold in Boston some years ago, in a miscellaneous lot of ornaments, were several Chinese porcelains. I anxiously awaited the day of sale, wondering who would be my competitors for these rare pieces. I was more than surprised at seeing not a soul who I believed knew what was to be sold: a beautiful Ming cream-white incense burner, standing ten inches high on four legs; a Tang cream-white horse with a tortoise-shell saddle, all of porcelain enamel; and a water buffalo, a Tang piece in dull white clay with its harness in dull faded colors, besides two women figures in clay and a bit of color on the cream-white drapery. Here were specimens found in the tombs of China which date back to the first modelling period of this ancient people in the Tang dynasty. Of course I secured them all.

I took two of the treasures with me this summer to London and exhibited them before the best expert in Europe. He assured me that they were absolutely genuine, and I was offered such prices for them that, like the true amateur collector, — I would not sell.

CHAPTER XVI

A ROYAL KLEPTOMANIAC

IT is only because of the recent death of a gentleman in Europe, whose name is well known throughout the civilized world, that I am at liberty to relate the interesting facts of an affair which, if known, would have startled the most exclusive society of the Continent.

In December of the year 188– two American gentlemen arrived in Nice, France, at Hotel des Anglais. One of these gentlemen was an invalid; the other myself. At dinner on the first night we noted that there were few Americans in the hotel, but many English and continental people. After dinner the gentlemen who were unaccompanied by ladies adjourned to the smoking room and, as they sat around a large open fire, those who spoke English joined in general conversation. One of the gentlemen sitting near me asked if I had seen the Hungarian nobleman, and on my replying that I had not, said he was the most interesting man in the hotel. He then told me that the young man was staying at Nice, although he went to Monte Carlo every morning, spent the entire day there, and returned to Nice at night. It was impossible, the Hungarian had said, for him to stay in Monte Carlo as he could not sleep there after the excitement of the day, and the Englishman said that he and the others had benefited from his return to Nice every night, as he related to them his exploits of the day.

On our way to Nice from Mentone, two days previous, we had stopped in Monte Carlo. My friend remained at the hotel while I went to the Casino. I tried my luck at the first table which greets the eye of the stranger, but, finding I lost continually, I gave it up and watched the other. After an hour I wandered through the different rooms, and at last stopped beside the table at which they were playing roulette for gold. Here only the large stakes were played — never less than a gold louis is placed on any

number; so making or losing becomes a
nervous strain upon the player.

One old lady, dressed in widow's weeds,
played a single louis at a time and seemed
to be gaining. A young man sitting beside
her was paid so much gold by the croupier
that he attracted my attention, and immediately I changed my position to watch him.
Presently he arose from the table and took
his gold with him.

When he stood up, his whole bearing was
different from that of any man in the room;
tall and slight, with a sallow complexion and
dark eyes, with a heavy, brown Vandyke
beard, he made himself the observed of all
observers. He was exquisitely dressed, and
the gems upon his fingers gave him the air
of a man of wealth. As he left the room, an
Englishman standing beside me turned and
said, "His earnings have been great." But
as it is not the custom to join in conversation
with strangers in the Casino, I soon walked
away and went back to the hotel.

Therefore, when the door of the smoking
room was opened that night at Nice, and the
Englishman who had been telling me of the

Hungarian nobleman exclaimed, "Here is the Hungarian now," I was much interested, as I recognized the gentleman whom I had seen two days previous playing roulette at the Casino. As he approached the fireplace the gentlemen moved in a larger semicircle so that he might draw his chair in nearer the fire. Then Sir Henry Mason, one of the Englishmen, asked him about his playing at Monte Carlo that day. He had been again successful and was very enthusiastic.

For several evenings he related that he had had the same luck each day, and on Monday night of the following week it was the general remark in the smoking room that the Hungarian nobleman had missed being present at dinner. One gentleman after another, as the evening came to its close, left the room, and I at last found myself alone. I lighted a fresh cigar to have a quiet smoke. Just as the clock struck half-past eleven the nobleman entered the room. His whole manner was changed; he threw himself on a leather-covered lounge and did not speak. After a few moments I laid my book aside on a little marble table, which was at my elbow, and said to him:

"Good evening; what is the matter?"
He sat up on the lounge and answered,
"Oh, a great deal. The fact is, I have lost
everything."

Turning to him I asked, "You do not mean
you have lost everything that you have?"

"Ah, no, not all that I have, but all that
I had with me. It is the same old story,
though, — very successful for a while, and
then one heavy loss."

He said that in his cool moments at home
he cautioned his bankers not to send him
more than fifteen thousand francs while
he was away, and to pay no attention to
what he might write or telegraph.

"To-day," he exclaimed, "I have telegraphed in my excitement, and they have not
answered; but they are right. I have been to
Cook's people, and they have offered to ticket
me through if I would give my watch and
other things as collateral. But while I might
do this, it would be mortifying. What I care
about is leaving Monte Carlo."

I began to moralize with him, to persuade
him to go home, but he laughed at me, and
in a few moments he left the lounge and,

taking a seat on the other side of the little white marble table near me, folded his arms, leaned forward and said:

"Would you lend me ten francs to-night?"

"Of course," I replied, taking two five-franc pieces from my pocket and placing them on the table. Whereupon he arose, and with the same dignity I had noticed in the Casino at Monte Carlo, said:

"I am a gentleman. I cannot take that money unless I give you something in exchange until I can pay you."

I laughed. "That is nonsense; ten francs amounts to nothing."

"Yes, but it amounts to a loan. Excuse me a moment." And, bowing, he left the room.

Presently he returned and, opening one of his hands upon the table, out fell a number of the most unique jewels. There was one scarfpin of two little men — one in gold and one in platinum — not more than one eighth of an inch in height, dressed as Esquimaux, and between them they were rolling a large diamond which represented a ball of ice. Others quite as odd were on the table, but that which attracted my attention most of all was a large piece of sardonyx. It was a stone one and a half inches long by three fourths of an inch wide, oval-shaped, and upon its surface was cut an intaglio of Actæon and the Hounds. I took this up and remarked:

"This is a beautiful stone; an antique."

"Yes, my grandfather gave it to my father, and my father to me. It is something I can never wear, but I always keep it by me."

It was a most wonderful red, and as I held it up to the light the figures, although cut in, stood out in bold relief, like a cameo. One side of the figure with the arm extended, holding tightly cords which held the hounds, had every muscle and ligament in the arm strained; while on the other side of the body, resting upon a long staff held in the hand, every muscle was in repose. As I stood up and held it before the light, I remarked again to him that it was a fine stone.

"Suppose you keep that," he answered, "you would like to look at it in the morning light, for in the daylight it is a deep orange instead of red, and is far more beautiful."

"Very well," I replied, "if you insist upon my taking something, I would like to look at the intaglio to-morrow, and then you can have it back."

He seemed to forget entirely its value, and taking up the other jewels in one hand, he grasped the two five-franc pieces in the other, and cried excitedly:

"Then the money is mine?"

He took a cigar from his pocket. "Take a cigar. I want to tell you what I am going to do with these ten francs. At the International Club, close by, there is a roulette table which is going all night. I cannot sleep, and therefore I will go in there and play." And standing up, he continued, "And I may make enough to go back to Monte Carlo to-morrow. Good night." And he left the room.

Shortly afterwards I retired, and in the morning when my friend and I came down to breakfast about ten o'clock, I went to the desk at the office and asked the Englishman who was in charge what had become of the

Hungarian. He did not at first seem to understand to whom I referred, but upon my explaining he said:

"Oh, that man? Some one was fool enough to loan him some money last night, and he went into the International Club and gambled all night. He was very fortunate and made several thousand francs. He returned here about five o'clock this morning, paid his bill, took his traps and went to Monte Carlo. He will not return."

"But," said I, "I was the one who loaned him the money last night, and he gave me something of value in return. As my friend and I are leaving for Florence on the three o'clock train this afternoon, I want to find him."

The clerk offered to telegraph to the Casino and principal hotels. "But," said he, "I do not think there is any chance of finding him, for the name he registered under here is probably assumed. Those fellows rarely register under their own names."

At intervals during the day I inquired whether he had received any reply, but he had nothing to tell me.

We went to Florence that afternoon, and after three months in Italy journeyed northward to Paris. My friend had left an order, previous to our going south, with a lapidary on the Rue de la Paix to cut a seal. One morning after our arrival we called at the shop, and my friend, who had insisted that my treasured antique was nothing but glass, urged me to show it to the lapidary and get his opinion. When the man looked at it through his glass, he started with deep emotion. "It is an antique of wonderful beauty! Where did you get it?" he asked. Not caring to go into particulars, I told him I had secured it in the south. On returning to New York, I again exhibited it to a connoisseur in antiques, and he made me such an astonishing offer that I wished more than ever I might find its rightful owner and return it to him. But I had no address; I simply had the last name and believed that he was a Hungarian. What his exact station in life was, I did not pretend to conjecture, and so for many years kept the stone.

Many years after I found myself in Europe with one of my nieces and passed many weeks in Rome. Having the intaglio with me one day, I took it to a famous engraver and lapidary on the Corso to ask his opinion of its age and if it were Greek.

After looking at it with intense curiosity he asked how I became possessed of it, and after I had related the story of the Hungarian, he called another man who also examined the stone. They asked if they might take a wax impression of it. After talking in an undertone for several minutes, the first man with whom I had spoken returned the gem and said:

"Yes, it is Greek — certainly a gem, a museum piece — " Then he abruptly asked, "Are you staying long in Rome?"

"For a month," I replied.

On reaching Rome we were the recipients of an invitation to be guests at a presentation at Court to Queen Margherita at the Quirinal Palace.

When the night came we were told by friends, long residents of Rome, that we should go to the Palace an hour before our invitation designated. When we arrived there, the door was opened by the Major-domo; we ascended the long staircase, which was covered with red velvet carpet, and banked on either side with pots of azaleas in full bloom. Halfway up there is a deep landing; here the staircase turns, and after twenty more steps we reached the long hall in which hundreds of lackeys, six feet tall or more, with powdered hair, and dressed in red velvet trimmed with gold lace, white satin knee breeches and white silk stockings, stood in waiting. One of them took our wraps and we followed other strangers down the long corridor to the room of mirrors, where the presentation was to take place.

The vast room, two or three stories high, with the beautiful Watteau decorations upon the walls of glass, was furnished around the sides with chairs upholstered in red satin. In the center of the room was a large divan beside which stood the Marchesa, who received us most cordially after our names were given by the gentlemen in waiting, who accompanied those to be presented. We joined the other Americans who stood at one side of the room, as persons of each nationality were placed together.

When all had assembled — some sixty in
number — the glass door at one side was
thrown open. The gracious Queen, the
gentlemen in waiting, and the Marchesa
entered. She spoke to each person in the
language of his country, and moved around
the room, entering into longer conversation
than just the formal greeting. As she was
leaving our particular party, she turned to
my niece and said, "You must ask the Marchesa what your uncle must do to have invitations to the great ball on Monday night
sent you."

After she left the apartment ices were
served, and the Marchesa came back to say
good night to each one. As we were leaving
the Marchesa, I asked what we should do to
secure invitations to the ball which the
Queen had spoken of. She said, "You can
call on me to-morrow at eleven; you will not
see me, but a young man, and he will receive
your cards for me."

The next day at eleven o'clock I drove to
the Quirinal Palace. I was received by the
young man. He asked me to accompany
him to a small room where, on a small table,

were two enormous books, — one bearing the crown with the name Umberto in gold letters beneath it, in which I entered my own name and address; and in the other book, which bore the name Margherita, I entered the name of my niece. That afternoon invitations for the great ball, stamped with the royal seal, were left at our hotel.

The ball surpassed in magnificence anything I had ever witnessed. Between two and three thousand people were present; but what astonished us most was that in the same room in which the presentation had taken place seats had been placed around three sides of the room — one above another — so that only a space was left in front of the throne large enough for one set to dance a quadrille. There was an open space on one side into an adjoining apartment, and exactly at the hour of eleven the orchestra, which was in a balcony high up on one side, played the Royal March of Italy, and the King entered, leading the Princess of Montenegro; the Crown Prince followed with his mother, Margherita. Then came the Crown Princess Helene and other royal persons. King

Humberto did not join in the quadrille, but royalty only took part in the dances which followed.

In an adjoining room ices were served, and the people wandered from one room to another until the ladies of the royal family, preceded by the gentlemen in waiting, passed through the assemblage, shaking hands with ladies on either side.

I had not noticed up to this time that we were observed. Most of the gentlemen present were in court dress and wore decorations. We, who wore the simple American evening dress, were few and far between. My niece, not having expected to go to such a royal function, had no jewels with her. I had suggested that she wear the intaglio which I had brought to Europe with me to show to Professor C—— at a museum in southern Italy, a connoisseur of the world on antiques. She seized the offer and wore the intaglio as a pendant at her neck. When we passed into the room where ices were being served, I noticed two gentlemen following us, who had been standing near us earlier in the evening. Without inquiry on my part one of them came forward and offered the information that, at the departure of the royal family from the room at one o'clock, the three banqueting rooms at the other side of the Palace would be thrown open for supper. The first room, he remarked, was for gentlemen accompanying ladies, the second for ladies alone, and the third for gentlemen alone.

When one o'clock arrived we passed through three long rooms banked with flowers at either side, and found ourselves in the supper room which was furnished with small tables for two or four persons. While sitting at a small table and partaking of supper, I was somewhat astonished to find that the two gentlemen who had given us the information were sitting at the next table, although not accompanied by ladies. While this passed through my mind I did not remark upon it, but, later on, in passing out through the flower rooms where each lady was given bunches of violets and azaleas, and on reaching the top of the grand staircase I again observed the two gentlemen who had spoken to me, and found they were closely following us to our carriage. Nothing more occurred to attract my attention to them, and we returned to the hotel.

Before leaving New York Mr. H——, an artist, had given me a letter of introduction to Professor C——, of a museum in southern Italy. As none of my friends wished to accompany me this time, I determined to go the day following the ball.

Upon my arrival I sent the letter of introduction to Professor C——, and received a most cordial note in return, appointing that afternoon at three o'clock for an interview. When I presented myself at the office of the museum I was taken through a long corridor to the professor's room. I knew that he would tell me the exact value and also perhaps the age of the antique which I had received many years before at the hands of the Hungarian, and was rather impatient to hear what he would say. Our conversation at first was upon the collection of antiques that was being made by prominent rich men in America, and also the collection which was in our Metropolitan Museum in New York.

"Have you been here before?" he asked. And on my telling him that I had been there several times he said, "Then you know the collection in the Gem Department?"

"Oh, very well," I replied, "and I do not know whether my friend in New York wrote you that I was particularly interested in intaglios."

"Yes," he replied, "he mentions the fact, and that you have collected some yourself. A number of years ago we had a curious incident in this museum during the visit of H. R. H., Prince —— of one of the Balkan principalities. It was before my time as professor, but it has never ceased to be a matter of wonderment to every one connected with the museum."

Upon my further inquiry he told me the following story:

During the visit of H. R. H., Prince ——, there was a special day set for him and his suite to visit the museum. Each portion of the museum through which they passed was shut off to the public while they examined that gallery. All the cases which are kept locked were thrown open that they might make a general inspection of the articles. In the room of intaglios they seemed to take particular interest, but, much to the astonishment of the curator and governors of the museum, when they departed, a famous intaglio was found to be missing. Inquiries were made among all those who had attended, but suspicion was fastened on no one in particular, and the only surmise was that some thief supposed to be of the party had accompanied the suite.

While we were discussing this matter, a messenger entered the room and gave him a telegram. As soon as the messenger had departed, the professor tore open the telegram, and upon reading the same started to his feet, exclaiming:

"This certainly is a curious coincidence." I looked up inquiringly, whereupon he added, "This telegram is from Rome, and informs me that the antique, of which we have been speaking, which was stolen so many years ago, has been discovered, and that arrests will be made this afternoon."

My thoughts can be more easily imagined than described. Questions presented themselves to me. Could my intaglio be the one? — Would they arrest me? — What explanation would they accept if I possessed the antique of great value? — Who was the stranger from whom I took it? I decided to be calm and ask questions.

"When the intaglio was stolen how many persons were with the Prince?" I asked.

"Oh, I do not know, it was so many years ago. There is an old man who was custodian of that part of the museum, who is still here, only in another department. I will send for him, as it is interesting now that there is a clue to finding the stone."

A messenger was sent to find the old man. The professor in the meantime questioned a clerk (who had entered and brought with him some papers) concerning the lost gem. Some of their conversation I could not hear.

"All I remember," said the clerk, "is that an old drawing of the lost antique hung for many years in this room, but that has disappeared." As he was speaking, he pulled out one drawer after another in the wall. "Here it is," he cried, passing him a small gilt frame which held a colored drawing.

"Yes, thank you. That will do. You may go."

When the door was closed, the professor examined the drawing for a while and then passed it to me, saying, "Do you care to see it?"

I felt confident what was coming. I was sure that if I looked at it I should betray myself. However, che professor was watching me, and I was obliged to examine it.

Certainly the surprise upon my face and the tone of my voice must have been apparent as I exclaimed:

"This the intaglio? Oh, you don't mean it. Why, this is Jupiter playing juggler with the sun, moon and stars."

"Yes. Why are you astonished? What did you expect was the subject?" he queried.

There was a knock at the door and the old custodian entered.

"You sent for me?"

"Yes, Camilo. You remember the intaglio which was lost so many years ago?"

"As if it were yesterday," answered the old man.

"You will be glad to know that it has been found," declared the professor.

"Found!" cried the custodian, rubbing his

hands together. "Then my prayers have been answered. Who took it?"

"Ah, we do not know yet. This gentleman is from America, and deeply interested in gems." Whereupon they both turned toward me.

The old man eyed me sharply and, whispering to his superior, he shambled down the room and opened an old secretary from which he took a large photograph mounted on pasteboard. Dusting it with his yellow handkerchief, he came back to where we sat. I saw that the photograph was of a group of men.

Without speaking a word they examined each face, then placing it on a shelf, went out. My suspicions were aroused and, leaning forward, I read the telegram as it lay on the desk:

"Antique intaglio found. Detain American who calls on you to-day."

This, then, was the reason he had sent for the custodian. The men grouped together in the photograph probably were H. R. H., Prince ——, and his suite. It had been examined by them to see if my face were there.

The two men at the ball in Rome had made inquiries at my hotel or of my friends, and had located me in southern Italy, and knew I was to call at the museum. These were my thoughts.

Why had the colored drawing of the intaglio, different from the one I possessed, been shown me? To allay my suspicions. I left my chair, and stood in front of the photograph on the shelf. One face was familiar; who was he?

Hearing footsteps of more than one person, I walked back to my chair. The door opened, and the professor, accompanied by an officer in uniform, entered.

"My dear sir," began my friend, "I am placed in a most trying position. You are my guest through this letter of introduction, and yet you are under suspicion by the Government."

"I understand you, except I cannot comprehend why you wished to deceive me."

"Deceive you? — How?"

"In showing me the colored drawing which is not of the intaglio which was stolen."

"Ah, how well you know," he cried in triumph.

"I do know, and you, sir, will apologize yet to me. First, let me ask you to allow me to speak to you alone."

He ordered the officer to stand outside the door; then, turning, waited for me to begin.

I told him the story of the Hungarian nobleman and of my obtaining the intaglio; how for many years I had kept it; of my niece wearing it at the ball the previous evening and my showing it to the lapidary on the Corso.

"Where is it now?" he inquired eagerly.

"In my pocket, but you cannot see it unless you show me evidence that it is the missing gem."

"Evidence! Why, sir, the officials who have just arrived saw it on your niece last night at the ball."

"Have you met them since they arrived?"

"No, but the officer, who is outside the door, has."

"Can you show me a drawing of the intaglio?" I ventured to ask.

"Yes." And taking the large photograph

of the group of men from the shelf, he turned it over, and there, attached to the back of the mount, was a drawing of Actæon and the Hounds.

"It is enough," said I, fully convinced, as I took the stone from my pocket and passed it to him. "No more proof is needed."

"Beautiful, wonderful," he said to himself, as he gazed upon it. "But how are you to prove you had it from a Hungarian nobleman at Nice?" Then, holding it under a magnifying glass, he added, "They will arrest you, and you will have to prove what you say."

"Will I?" And, taking up the photograph, I inquired, "Who is this man?" placing my finger on the center figure in the group of men.

"That man? H. R. H., Prince ——."

"Impossible!" I stammered.

"Why impossible?" he asked.

"Because he is the man to whom I loaned the ten francs."

"Hush! Do not speak so loudly; he must be protected," whispered the professor, grasping my arm.

Then seating himself, he said in a half-audible voice, "H. R. H., Prince ——, a royal kleptomaniac."

The embarrassing explanations which would be necessary if the intaglio were returned to its place in the museum and the possible connection of the Prince of a neighboring Balkan principality with the disappearance of the gem would certainly create a scandal that all public officials shrink from, so after due consideration it was decided not to take the intaglio or accept it from me; furthermore, they preferred to drop the whole matter and would not admit that they had any interest in the gem.

Therefore the intaglio remains in my possession.

CHAPTER XVII

THE GERMAN SPIRIT

AN American can hardly conceive what must have been the state of mind of the German who the day following the *Lusitania* horror mailed to a former acquaintance (an American) in Switzerland one of the original copper medals commemorating the event. The date on the medal is May *fifth*, instead of the *seventh*, the date of the disaster, showing the premeditation on the part of those in authority. Of course the American recipient was horrified to believe his former German acquaintance should presume that an American would care to have such a medal.

Before a week had passed, the German people realized how they had shocked the whole civilized world by their perfidy and instructed the general public to recall any of these medals which had been sent out of

Germany. The American in Switzerland received a request that he return the medal
which he had sent him, but he was able to
answer that it had already been sent to the
United States and that thereafter all acquaint-
anceship must end between them. The medal
was sent to me, and on the front is depicted
the ship sinking, and on the reverse side is
the office of the Cunard line with Death
selling tickets of passage.

At the first battle of the Marne, when the
Germans were retreating, a German general
lay dying on the field as the French came up
in pursuit.

A Frenchman went to the dying German
general and knelt at his side, supporting the
head of the unconscious man. When he had
breathed his last, the Frenchman undid his
coat to ascertain his name, if possible.

Upon the inner coat hung the Iron Cross of
the highest order, — iron bound in silver hung
from a black ribbon edged with white. On
one side of the cross are the initials F. W. 1813,
the year the Iron Cross was first inducted by
Frederick William, the Kaiser's grandfather.

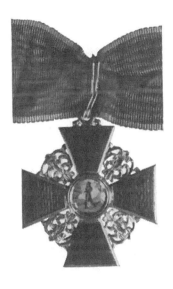

CROSS OF ST. ANNE
OF RUSSIA

IRON CROSS
First order of Germany,
with pins attached to ribbon

On the other side is W—— 1914, the year when presented to the wearer.

On the ribbon were two enameled pins: one with the center of red enamel with the star and crescent in white (Turkey) and around it a border of the German and Austrian colors, bearing the words in gold, "Gott strafe England"; the other, a round enameled pin bearing three flags — Germany, Austria and Turkey — flying across a map of Italy surrounded by the blue sea, and the inscription, "Gott strafe den Treubruch" (God strike the traitor), of course meaning Italy when she left the Entente.

To-day Germans assert that no such pins were made or worn by officers or men, but here is the proof.

The Frenchman bestowed the Iron Cross and the pins upon my friend in Switzerland, who gave them to me for my collection.

CHAPTER XVIII

ROMANCE OF THE SILVER CLASP

TEN years ago, in the Holy City of Kairouan, twenty-six miles south of Tunis, the last of the cities of Tunisia to come under the Protectorate of France, I was wandering through the streets, gazing at the marvelous mosques of white marble glistening in the sunshine (there are over eighty of these mosques, some large and some small), when my attention was attracted to a number of Dervishes or holy men performing their strange antics in a side entrance to the Mosque of the Barber, before a crowd of Arabs who seemed lost in admiration of the feats which were contrary to all human beliefs. They held scorpions, alive and wriggling, above their heads, and then these holy men would open their mouths and drop the green and brown scorpions into them and swallow them without any apparent discomfiture, while the motley crowd looked on admiringly, convinced that these men were truly holy and protected by their religion from any harm.

"It's a strange sight," a voice said, and turning I beheld a young Arab standing close to me.

"You cannot understand it; neither can I," he continued in English.

The young man was dressed differently from any other person in the assemblage. He wore a fez on his head, but his long coat, which fitted him perfectly, was of beautiful light-blue spun silk, and down the front, not more than an inch apart, were many small silk-covered buttons of a deep magenta color.

"Have you been inside the mosque?" he asked.

"No," I replied. "I have just come from Tunis and there no one but Mohammedans are allowed to enter a mosque."

"I know, but it is different here. Come in out of this glare and heat. I will show you around," rejoined the Arab.

We moved to the front entrance and then

entered the mosque. The size and great aisles were bewildering. Hundreds of beautifully fashioned pillars supported the great Moorish arches, ——some pillars of marble, some of porphyry, and others of jasper, but I could not help remarking, "The pillars seem to be all Roman in style and design."

"Yes," he replied. "Thirteen hundred years ago, when Sidi Okba founded this Holy City of Kairouan, the city of Carthage was despoiled of all its marbles and they were brought here and were used in building all the mosques and the great city wall."

As we traversed the great building he asked about America. He told me he had been in England twice, and I found him well versed in English history and literature.

At noon I begged him to lunch with me and in the afternoon we visited many curious parts of the city I should never have seen by myself.

He took me to a café where possibly twenty men could be served at a time. In the center was one large marble slab which served as a table and at which all the patrons sat.

"This table is peculiar," he remarked.

"Over a thousand years ago there lived a man of great riches for that time who told his friends that he had a plan to perpetuate his name and have men in Kairouan speak of him every day, even a thousand years after his death. It was at last revealed when he died that he had built this café, and the great table of marble was to be his tomb and his name is cut into the stone. The café was endowed and ever since has been a great source of income to the mosque, which is the recipient of the rental. The café has never been closed a day and is always well patronized, and the name of the donor is forever on the lips of those who frequent the place."

My Arab friend, after a few days' acquaintance, said he had sent word to his father who lived ten miles from Kairouan toward Sfax that he wished to bring me to their home and show me a real Arab house. A runner had brought back word that I would be welcome.

We went by rail to a small station where we were met by an ox team drawing a two-wheeled cart, upon the floor of which was a heavy mattress. After each of us, lying full length on the mattress, made ourselves comfortable, we started for a four-mile ride to the Arab's home.

When we entered the grounds of the place by a road which was bordered on either side with great date palms standing forty feet high, we were met by men with drums and curious wind instruments. who escorted us to the house or houses — for there was a collection of not less than ten dwellings — in the center of which stood the great house in which the father dwelt.

My friend left me at his father's doorway and said it was not etiquette for him to enter with me, his father's guest. He must go to his own house and would see me later. Upon entering the house, a servant took off my shoes and hose and washed my feet, then put white silk sandals on my feet and carried away my hose and shoes.

Presently a major-domo came and led me through a long hall and into a small room.

Reclining on a couch was my host, a fine-looking Arab with snow-white beard and dressed in a long garment of plum-colored silk lined with light yellow. He bowed most courteously and motioned me to sit or recline on a couch opposite.

Much to my astonishment he spoke excellent English and asked me about America. Then without a change or expression he said, "What can you tell me about Tel. and Tel. stock?"

I was thunderstruck.

Then he explained.

"My broker in Paris, who advises me, some years ago recommended me to invest in Tel. and Tel.; so I did and it turned out well. I only fear that some day they may invent something better."

My assurance seemed to please him, and we drifted into the usual conversation of two people from the opposite ends of the world.

I inquired how he became so conversant with everything English.

This led to his telling me the following story:

"Thirty years ago," he began, "a young Englishman, an artist, came to Tunis to sketch. In the old Arab quarter, in the *souks* or narrow streets where the Arab shops are situated, the young artist sketched unmolested but surrounded by a curious crowd. A young woman, veiled so only her eyes were visible, was standing near and watched the young man. Day after day she came, and at last the Englishman noticed her and found she could speak French. She was very shy and at first would not reply to his questions.

"At that time, thirty years ago, it was dangerous for a foreigner to address any woman of the better class, but the artist was very anxious for this young woman to allow him to paint her picture, — of course veiled. She would not consent. However, a shopkeeper of beautiful silks and embroideries from whom the artist had purchased many pieces of his stock told the artist he would use his best endeavors with the girl. One day it was arranged that the artist should go to an inner room in the shop. The young woman was there and allowed him to make a sketch of her. Day after day they met in the shop, and evidently she was quite as fascinated as he, for much to his surprise, when alone with him one day, she threw off her veil and he beheld her face for the first time. The burnous or cloak she wore fell to the ground; the silver clasp and chain which held it at the neck had given way. The artist on his knees told her she was the fairest creature he had ever seen, and that he was madly in love with her.

"She acknowledged her interest in him but said she was mad to have shown him her face, and that if the people at the mosque opposite knew it they would kill her. She veiled quickly and said that they must not meet again and that as she was a Mohammedan she never should have spoken to him. As she finished veiling, the shopkeeper appeared but was unaware of what had happened. The Englishman placed the burnous over her shoulders and spoke of the beautiful clasp and chain of silver which held the cloak together at her throat.

"She told him it was an antique silver clasp three hundred years old and very rare. He begged her to return the following morning, but she shook her head. From his inner pocket he took a Testament which his mother had given him when he left England, and pressed it into her hand. She took it and fled.

"Months passed, and day after day the

artist came to the *souks*, but she was nowhere to be seen. The shopkeeper feigned ignorance and said all he knew was that she had gone away.

"Kairouan was not then under the protectorate of France, and the marvelous stories of its great beauty reached the ears of every foreigner, although no one but Mohammedans were allowed to enter the city. Several who had tried had lost their lives or had never been heard of again.

"The artist decided that he would journey south and behold the Holy City from afar.

"One night he lay in the sand outside the great wall, so as to see the wondrous sight in the morning when the sun broke through the dawn and shone upon the white and gilded domes of the mosques. He noticed that creeping slowly to his side was a man he thought an Arab, who whispered to him in French.

"He learned that the man was not an Arab but a French spy disguised as one. He told the Englishman he was going to enter at the big gate with the Arab market gardeners at dawn, and urged the artist to join him, only cautioning him it was at the risk of his life.

"The Englishman watched all night for an Arab leaving the city from whom he could purchase clothes. At last he was successful and quickly covered his own clothes with those bought from the Arab. The Frenchman produced a bottle containing walnut juice, and the artist stained his face, neck and hands, becoming to all appearances an Arab.

"As soon as the streaks of dawn were visible, the market gardeners, with their heavily ladened donkeys, bestirred themselves and moved toward the great gate of the city which would soon open for the day.

"The Frenchman and artist mingled with the crowd and thus hoped to escape detection from the Mohammedan guards at the entrance to the Holy City. Once inside, they believed they would be safe. They entered, seemingly without being observed, but it was the unalterable custom of all Mohammedans to proceed at once to one of the mosques and fall on their knees in prayer. Their neglect to do this attracted attention, and they were watched, for the Arab of Kairouan was suspicious of all strangers.

Presently they were seized and their disguise was discovered. Later they were taken before the judges and examined. The Frenchman was immediately cast into prison, but the Englishman pleaded his cause as wholly innocent, and that he only desired to sketch and paint. One of the judges became interested and said he would become responsible for him if left in his care. Whereupon he was seated at one side of the room until the court adjourned, but two guards were placed on either side of him.

"After the noon hour he was taken to the judge's house and locked into a room on the second floor. As he entered the room, he saw that the guards took up their positions at the foot of the staircase.

"Food was sent to him and, not having slept the night before, he fell into a deep sleep. It was dark when he awakened, but by the light of a single candle he discovered some one had entered and left another supply of food and water. After a while the noise in the street below, on which the house backed, quieted down and he again slept.

"Long after midnight he was awakened

by some one gently touching his arm. In the dim candlelight he saw the judge leaning over him and heard him whisper:

"'At the first streak of dawn, open the shutter of your window which opens on the back street. You will find a rope fastened to the iron work; let yourself down. A boy with two donkeys will be in the street. Mount one of the donkeys and follow the boy out of the great gate. He will know the way after you are outside.'

"The artist was bewildered and did not know whether to believe the judge or not. The judge, seeing him falter, quickly unbuttoned his coat and laid bare his chest and held the candle close to his breast. Just above his heart was tattooed the cross and as he covered himself again he murmured, 'I believe.'

"Life and hope immediately sprang into the artist's heart. He clasped the hand of the judge and pressed it. Not a word was spoken. Then he knew he was alone; the judge had vanished.

"The first rays of gray dawn appeared and, opening the shutters quietly, he found the rope and lowered himself to the ground.

The donkeys and the boy were there; he mounted one donkey and they started.

"It was much easier going out of the great gate than entering, as no guards made examination or inquiry. The boy did not offer to speak and did not reply when questioned in English or French.

"When they had proceeded a long distance from the city, the artist threw away the Arab clothes which had covered his own and lay down in the shade of a group of palms and fell asleep. The afternoon was well passed when he awakened and found the boy had set out food and drink for them. After they had eaten, they again started on their journey.

"Late in the afternoon they reached this house where we are now," said my host, "but the judge had by a quicker and shorter route arrived before them.

"The Arab boy, on entering this very room, let fall the dark cloak of burlap which had covered him since they started on the donkeys from Kairouan, stripped off his turban, and the Englishman stood amazed before the girl whose picture he had painted in the *souk* of Tunis.

"The white burnous was still clasped at the neck with the cut-silver chain and clasp. The judge explained that the girl was his niece, and when she fled from Tunis she had come to him at Kairouan. She had shown him the Testament and told him of the man who had given it to her. Then for the first time the old judge revealed to her his own belief in Christianity but cautioned her to tell no one. He then taught her English so she could read the Testament and she accepted the faith too.

"Now they both claimed it was a miracle which had brought the Englishman to Kairouan.

"As soon as preparations could be made, the artist was sent to Malta and later the judge followed with his niece; in Malta the artist and the Arab girl were married in the English church and went from there to England to live."

My host arose from his couch and opened a small box inlaid with mother-of-pearl and silver, and from it he took the cut-silver chain and clasp.

"This is all I have left of the Romance "

and then, going to the doorway and assuring himself that no one was listening, he added, "I was the judge and I have kept the faith. See." He stripped open his inner coat and bared his breast and there, tattooed above his heart, was the cross.

The old man had won my admiration and two days later, when I bade him farewell, he smiled and pressed into my hand a small package which afterwards I found contained the curiously cut antique chain and clasp.

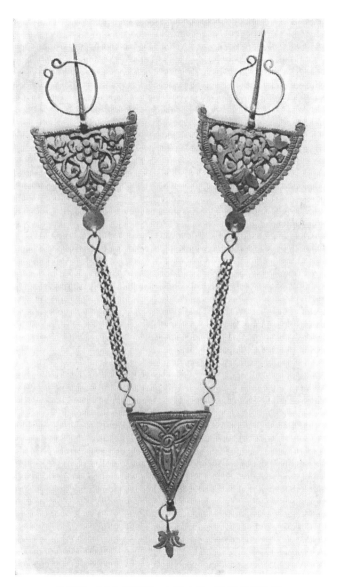

CUT SILVER ARAB BUCKLE
Seventeenth Century

CHAPTER XIX

A VALUABLE FIND

MY friend, Mr. C——, was living in Liverpool in 1910 as agent of an American Exporting Company. Week-ends his wife and he would motor to different points of interest in England. An acquaintance who was an artist wrote them from B——, in the center of England, that he and his wife had rented an old abbey and asked them to pass a few days with them.

When my friend and his wife arrived, they found the old abbey in an almost perfect state of preservation. The artist told him that after sketching the abbey and exploring it many times they inquired of the overseer if the place could be rented. He assured them that the lord of the manor would certainly be pleased to find a tenant, but that no one would take it, as there was no way of heating the rooms, which were large. They

were offered the abbey and ten acres of land
around it for £60 a year, on a lease of five
years. The artist's wife, who had been in
Canada, immediately sent out to Montreal
for piping and a heater of large size. After
the heating apparatus was installed, the family
took possession.

Mr. C—— said that when they were taken
into the old refectory for dinner, he exclaimed
on seeing the hangings on the walls. The artist told this story about them:

One day he was driving some miles from
Kidderminster when he was overtaken by a
rainstorm of great severity. Seeing ahead of
him a large stone barn with a driveway leading to it, he drove as fast as possible toward
it. The farmer, seeing him, threw open the
great doors of the barn so he could drive inside. When the artist got out of his open
wagon, the farmer took his coat and hat
and carried them into the kitchen of the
house to dry.

The artist noticed that the old barn had
no windows and the only light came in from
the opening of the doors. Hung around the
inside walls were heavy squares of what

seemed to be burlap, but on feeling them he found them to be made of wool and very heavy. When the farmer came back the artist inquired, "What is this on the walls of your barn?"

"I don't know. It's been here ever since we bought the place forty years ago. No, it's not burlap," he answered.

The artist, after his eyes had become accustomed to the darkness, said he could see the outline of figures and bits of faded color upon the surface of the hangings.

He remarked to the farmer, "You know where the old abbey is. Now I have some large wall space to cover in the old refectory, and I would like these four pieces if you will sell them to me."

"I'd sell them to you, but they keep out the cold and wind that comes into the barn through the chinks in the stonework. I'd have to fill and cement those holes in the wall," replied the farmer.

However, after much bargaining, the artist paid the farmer £6 for the four hangings. They took them down and folded them and piled them into the back of the wagon.

When the artist arrived at the abbey his wife refused to have the hangings brought inside as they were so dirty and smelly, so the next morning they were spread out on the grass. Sure enough, they were, as he had supposed, tapestries, but in a terrible condition, dirty, riddled with holes in the borders, stained and apparently worthless.

The artist wrote to the Gobelin works in France and inquired if they would clean and repair them. They replied to send the pieces and they would estimate the cost of reclamation. From Kidderminster the artist procured packing cases and sent the tapestries to the Gobelin works.

The estimate came back that it would cost £100 to put them in condition and that they were worth saving, as they were Flemish tapestries over three hundred years old. One hundred and twenty-five pounds was all the artist had, but he advanced the £100 and waited. When they were returned, these wonderful tapestries were placed on the walls of the refectory and charmed the eyes of my friend, Mr. C——.

A year later Mr. C—— again visited the

artist, but behold, — the tapestries were gone. Upon inquiry he discovered that a short time after his last visit the lord of the manor died, and as the lease of the abbey was near expiration, it could not be rented again. The abbey must be sold and its ten acres of land. The price was stated, — £3000. The artist was in despair. Finally he sent for Christie's man to come from London to see the tapestries and value them.

Christie gave £7000 for the four tapestries. The artist bought the abbey and land for £3000 and salted down the £4000. But upon the walls of the refectory is an interesting collection of old, faded, rose-colored draperies bought at a sale of the furnishings of D—— Castle in 1913.

CHAPTER XX

THE TALISMAN

A PROFESSOR in a college near Boston, previous to the War, made with his wife an annual trip to Europe, sailing each year on a steamer that would land them at a port near their objective.

In 1906 they landed at Queenstown and not being blessed with an overabundance of money they followed their usual custom of hiring a horse and wagon to journey through Ireland. They were not bound to trains, and the only route they avoided was that in the published book for automobilists.

The professor told me of the many happy and interesting experiences that he and his wife had. Therefore I repeat the following, as the professor's wife was an amateur collector of curious necklaces.

One night they came to a tidy inn where they were made most comfortable. In the morning they asked the innkeeper if there were any old castle or church near, to which they could drive. He said that about fifteen miles away were the ruins of an old castle, built in the fifteenth century. One part of the keep was still inhabited by the descendants of the family. These old people were very glad to show the ruins and be paid a trifle for their services, as they were desperately poor. It all awakened the travelers' curiosity, and as the innkeeper said that they could not see the castle and get back in time for lunch, the professor and his wife ordered a basket of good things to eat for four people, and a good bottle of wine. The basket was put into the back of the wagon and the two started on their adventurous drive to the castle. The fifteen miles faded away and soon they could see the castle on a hill in the distance.

A small boy opened a gate at the foot of the driveway which led up to the ruins. From a doorway in a turret of the structure came an old man who bade them welcome. Soon his wife appeared with a bunch of large keys. They certainly were not hirelings, but

the Lord and Lady of the Manor. Their
poverty had not robbed them of graciousness
and they spoke of everything connected with
the castle with the declaration of ownership.

They were quite as quaint as the ruins
and told at last of the noble deeds of their
ancestors. At noon the old lady apologized
for not being able to ask them to lunch and
gave them to understand that she was hin-
dered by the lack of help and did not intimate
that it was because they could not afford to
have company. The professor's wife, a most
tactful person, laughingly said, "When we
left the inn at D——, not knowing when we
would return, we had a hamper of food put
into the wagon, and it would be most romantic for us if you would let us spread a
cloth in the keep enclosure and join us in
a picnic lunch, for we have more than
enough."

A flush of excitement passed over the old
lady's face, and as the professor undid the
hamper his wife took out a tablecloth and
soon they were all at work. Afterward they
sat down on the grass and were helped most
bountifully to chicken and duck and salad

and fruit, topped off with the bottle of wine.

The old couple told how fifty-five years before, when they were married in the village church, the wedding party had all come to the castle and spread the wedding feast in just the same spot. She asked many questions about America, and the professor's wife told her how they made a journey each year to some place that they had planned to visit and had read about during the previous winter evenings. After the meal was finished, a new friendship seemed to have started between the two ladies and the professor's wife confidentially told her hostess of her weakness for necklaces and that she had quite a collection.

The "Lady of the Castle" said, "We have an old necklace that I will show you. It has been in the family for three hundred years."

She left her guests and entered the castle. The necklace she brought back with her was of curious beaten silver of a most unusual design, from which hung a pendant larger than an ordinary sized locket. As she passed it to her visitor, she remarked, "The pendant has a black stone in the center that has always been said to be a talisman. You will notice what is engraved on the other side."

Turning it over were these words,

"The wolf will never come to the door
of him who owns this charm."

The professor and his wife were greatly interested in this relic of the sixteenth century. Later in the afternoon, as they were preparing to go back to the inn, the professor's wife gave her address to the old "Lady of the Castle" and told her if she ever decided to part with the necklace and pendant to write her and she would buy it if the price were not too large. Whereupon the old couple withdrew to the door of the tower in consultation. At last the old lady came forward and said, "If you will give me five pounds for the necklace and pendant, you can have it now."

With the true amateur collector's hesitation, the professor's wife took the antique chain and pendant and without a word opened her purse, from which she took five pounds. Passing it to the old lady she asked for a written receipt which was promptly given. Farewells were said and they departed.

The professor said his wife wore this necklace and told the story to many people.

When Christmas came they went to New York to pass the holidays. There was a wedding present that had to be given later, so Mrs. Professor went to one of the large jeweller's to buy a piece of silver. The same elderly man from whom she had bought silver in the past waited on her. Presently he inquired about the old necklace and the curious pendant attached to it. She told him the story. He asked if he could examine it, and as she handed it to him, he called another salesman to wait on her and withdrew into a small room.

When he returned he remarked, "I was showing this to one of our partners, and he wishes to know if you would mind coming into the small room and allowing one of our men to unscrew the five minute screws that hold the back on to this pendant, for we do not think that the talisman is a black stone." She, of course, assented.

When the workman unscrewed and took

off the back of the pendant the black stone fell out, but proved to be the largest black pear-shaped pearl the jewellers affirmed they had ever seen. The professor's wife was amazed.

"It would be wholly unsafe for you to take this back to the hotel," said the jeweller. "Leave it with us and we will give you a receipt for it. Then you and your husband come in to-morrow and we will tell you more about its value."

She left it there and hurried to the hotel to tell the professor.

The following morning they saw the jeweller and were told of the immense value of the pearl and that the inscription on the back,

"The wolf will never come to the door
of him who owns this charm"

proved true.

The jeweller would not take the pearl to sell, but would give so many thousand dollars outright for it.

The professor and his wife did not hesitate. They had never had such a sum of money in their lives, so they were promptly given a cashier's check. The day after they reached Cambridge, they sent the little old "Lady of the Castle" a draft for ten thousand dollars and wrote her a note telling her that truly the pendant contained a talisman and that no wolf would ever come to her door.

CHAPTER XXI

A LOST ART

OVER forty years ago a friend and I traveled from Florence, Italy, to Perugia. In the first-class railway carriage was an Italian gentleman who spoke English fluently and was much interested in our observations on his country. I chanced to mention my admiration of King Humberto and his devotion to the poor people of Rome who had been attacked by a plague like cholera.

"Yes," said the Italian, "he is truly a King — I have just been at Rome consulting the Government in regard to our own people in my town, many of whom have been stricken with the plague." From his conversation I realized he was carrying a great burden.

Branching off from this subject, he asked if I had been in Gubbio in the hills.

"It is worth visiting," he said, "for, you

know, it was the seat of the best Italian
majolica in the fifteenth century. One Giorgio
Andreoli, who produced this most beautiful
faience, made some most remarkable colors
of ruby tint; and there is a legend that on
one occasion, when a child of his was stricken
with the plague, he vowed that if God would
spare his child's life he would make it his
life's work to produce a color on majolica
which by its fame would bring a large increase
in income that he would devote to Holy
Church. The child recovered, — and true
to his word Andreoli cast his treasures of
pure gold into the melting pot and the famous
ruby tint was the outcome.

"It remained a secret which was handed
down to his sons, — but was afterwards lost
and only recovered by Angelica Fabbri in
1853."

Of course I was more than interested and
asked many questions.

The gentleman remarked "that at the death
of the sons of Andreoli, who carried their secret with them, the faience makers of Gubbio
found that they must do something to keep
their majolica above the average of that

manufactured in other Italian towns. So during the sixteenth century they improved in drawing and colors, rivalling all competitors. The best examples are in the Bargello Museum in Florence. Gubbio only possesses one piece of Andreoli, a *tazza* with St. Francis receiving the stigmata."

"You must be a collector," I said, "for your enthusiasm and knowledge are indicative of that craving a man who collects possesses."

"Yes, I have a few pieces and to tell you the truth, I would willingly starve for a long period to own more," he answered.

Finding we were approaching the place where I must change trains, I asked to be allowed to contribute toward the relief of his plague-stricken townspeople. At first he refused, saying he was a stranger to me and I did not know that he was to be trusted.

He accepted my gift when I assured him of my confidence in him as he was a gentleman and a collector.

We exchanged visiting cards. His bore a coronet and confirmed my estimate of him.

When we parted, my friend Lamson continued the journey to his destination, to meet me later at Perugia.

Lamson and the Italian became such friends that Lamson was invited to be his guest while in Pavia. A few days later, I was summoned to proceed at once to Pavia, as Lamson was quite ill.

The castle was on the outskirts of the city. The stone pile stood on a hill which was approached by a winding avenue with a double row of dark green cedar trees on either side. One hundred feet below the castle was a plaza with a tiled floor, and a balustrade of stone guarded the precipitous side toward the valley. The one hundred and fifty stone steps leading up to the main entrance were covered with green moss. The door was a foot thick, studded with iron knobs and secured on the inside by a grill of steel.

The servant who admitted me was a humpback. I was met in the hall by my host, who assured me that my friend was better, although three nights before he had been in high fever.

"I immediately sent for my priest, who is an excellent doctor," said the Count, "and he stayed in attendance all night. A nun from a neighboring hospital has been installed to take charge of the patient, so he will recover soon."

"Does the doctor think he is seriously ill?" I inquired.

"Not now — but one can never tell what is behind fever and a chill," he replied.

I was not allowed to see Lamson, as we thought it might alarm him if he thought I had been sent for. In a week he had so recovered that the priest-doctor advised his being removed to Perugia.

While I stayed in the castle, I wandered through the many rooms, admiring the pictures, majolica and armor which hung on the blackened walls. It was before the days of lighting by electricity, consequently the apartments were lighted with candles in hanging black-iron chandeliers and in silver sconces on the walls. In the corners of the refectory were iron tripods holding dozens of tapers, while on the long table were silver candelabra. Great flagons of silver filled the niches around the walls. All of past glory —

The Count himself had the extreme eastern

rooms painted in white and furnished in
modern style. His whole manner during
Lamson's illness was different than when we
first met. He never went near Lamson's
rooms, but the doctor reported to him in his
apartment night and day. But during the
two weeks we were in Perugia, we received
daily visits from the Count, who had resumed
his charming manners. At last we bade him
farewell and proceeded to Geneva.

The doctor came every day to Perugia,
but I did not know until later that he had
made a confidant of my friend Lamson.

It seems in years before the Count had been
most dissipated, and his wife had been obliged
to leave him, — not divorced but separated.
She had, upon leaving him, entered a convent
and later devoted herself to nursing in the
Church hospital.

When Lamson was taken so ill and the
doctor told the Count a nurse must be
procured at once, the only one available was
the Countess. The doctor implored her to
attend, and she came on condition that she
would not meet the Count. This accounted
for his change in manner. The priest added

that the Count had reformed soon after his wife left him and had become very charitable, aiding the sick, and whenever he found in the town deformed or humpback people, he made a place for them as servants at the castle.

We returned to America, and Lamson kept up a correspondence with the priest-doctor.

Two years later the Count died, and the priest secured two pieces of seventeenth-century majolica from the Count's collection for me — one depicting Venus ascending to heaven from the sea; the other, Bacchus offering grapes to a goddess — both wonderful examples of majolica of Gubbio.

GUBBIO ITALIAN MAJOLICA
Seventeenth Century

CHAPTER XXII

A COLONIAL COLLECTION

IN an old house in Woburn, Massachusetts, some twenty years ago, lived an old bachelor, Elijah, ninety years old. Ever since his mother had died, thirty years before, he had been the sole occupant of the house.

Next door, not ten feet away on the north side, was the house of a relative, and for the thirty years, three times a day, this relative's wife had put the meals through the kitchen window for the old man. He was a cousin of my grandmother, and out of curiosity more than anything else from boyhood up I would go to Woburn and call upon him about every four months.

During his life I never got into the main part of the house. He had an office in the back of the house and received every one there. A large stove stood in the center of this room and a pile of wood was near the door. An old crony of his occupied an old Windsor chair on one side of the stove and Elijah the one opposite. Day after day and night after night they sat in these chairs and talked and slept, for they rarely went to bed. I can remember, as a boy, how I used every artifice to induce Elijah to admit me to the other rooms of the house, but it was of no avail. He used to say, "No one has crossed the threshold of that hall since my mother died."

My grandmother had been brought up in that house, as she was an orphan and had been taken there by her aunt. She had told me that in wardrobes in the house were silk and velvet dresses that would stand alone, and furniture that was made before the Revolution, — the best examples of colonial designs. She also said there were trunks filled with men's short clothes and ruffled shirts of the eighteenth century.

I tried to screw my courage up to asking Elijah about these family relics, but if the conversation drifted toward the contents of the house, he would change the subject.

One day he told me why he never married; I afterwards told the story to the son-in-law of the late Honorable Thomas Nelson Page, and Mr. Page wrote it into a short story called "The Bigot," which was published in *Harper's Magazine*.

Just before Elijah's death I asked him to tell me if the dresses and trunks with short clothes were in the house.

He hesitated and then said, "Some years ago our clergyman one Sunday made a plea for clothes for the Michigan sufferers, and I packed up all those old things and sent them."

My heart sank, for I knew I could never find my ancestors' clothes. Strange to say, some time after that I was in Detroit, and at dinner one evening told this story of the old clothes, whereupon two ladies said they were on the committee who received the things from the East and they remembered perfectly well what a commotion was aroused when several brass-studded, hair-covered trunks were received and found to contain dresses and short clothes, shoes and buckles, ruffled shirts, dainty laces. One of the ladies stated that the committee concluded they would be of no use to the sufferers from Michigan's great fire, but decided to put them up at auction, as many ladies wished to buy them. They brought tremendous prices and aided the sufferers in that way.

Elijah and his friend sat as usual one night beside the stove. His friend told me afterward that in the middle of the night it grew so cold that he wakened, and as it was Elijah's turn to put on wood, he called to him, but Elijah did not answer.

"I walked across to Elijah's chair. There he was, sitting a little forward, his chin dropped on his chest. I put on some wood and then took his woolen scarf, which hung on a nail on the wall, and tied up his chin, and then I went back to my chair and went to sleep."

"Sleep?" I inquired. "Could you sleep?"

"Oh, yes, I'm ninety years old myself and when a man is my age, passing on seems so natural that you don't mind," he replied.

After a few days the house was cleaned, and we could see the furniture, — all very simple, either mahogany or white birch. A mahogany cabinet contained one hundred and eight pieces of old blue and white Staffordshire china with the name of "Wood Bros." stamped on the bottom of each piece; the china was the sparrow pattern, with the bird in the center of each, and not a piece was broken or chipped; there were a dozen plates of the mother teaching her boy to read from a book laid out on her knees; a dozen or more historical plates, with Paine's views of the State House and Harvard College and one of Lafayette on the balcony of the old house at the corner of Park and Beacon streets; sandwich glass in plates and saucers, and tea sets of Spode and Chelsea ware.

A chest of black oak was locked and had to be broken open, as no key could be found. It contained articles wrapped in Boston newspapers of 1826, probably the last time it was opened. There was a rifle with a silver plate sunken in the butt with the date 1769 and Elijah's grandfather's name engraved upon it. Fifty-one inches was the length of the barrel. On the paper around it was written, "This gun carried to the battle of Lexington by Elijah Wyman." In another package was the powderhorn with a wooden stopper and on a piece of paper was written, "Powder carried to battle of Lexington", and with it was the bullet mold. At the bottom of the chest was the blue homespun swallow-tail coat with silver buttons which Elijah Wyman wore at that memorable battle. In a small bundle were found a pewter pitcher and two pewter mugs and marked on the paper, "These were used by Mrs. A. Wyman, who lived on the line between Lexington and Bedford and who hid Hancock and Adams in her barn the night before the battle of Lexington. She served them beer during the night in these mugs and carried the beer in this pitcher; also gave them a cooked salmon." What relics of the past!

These are all in a glass case in the Old State House in Boston, and were given by the writer to the Bostonian Society in memory of young Gresham of Indiana, the first American boy to fall on the field of France in the Great War, thus linking the two great battles together.

In an iron box in the house was a *New York Evening Post* newspaper of 1784, containing the farewell speech to the American Army by George Washington, delivered at Newburg, New York. This newspaper is framed and is in the Harvard Club library in Boston.

The fact that this house remained practically closed for fifty years and that no one saw this unique collection was really most fortunate, for under ordinary circumstances the different articles would not have been kept as a whole. They now furnish a great object lesson to the many visitors to the Old State House.

END

INDEX

187